LARGE PRINT
Super #4
CROSSWORDS

Published by Playmore Inc., Publishers,
230 Fifth Avenue, New York, N.Y. 10001
and Waldman Publishing Corp.,
570 Seventh Avenue, New York, N.Y. 10018

Printed in Canada

PUZZLE 1

ACROSS

1. Changing hide into leather
5. Reef substance
10. Pro __; proportionately
14. Medicinal herb
15. Solitary
16. Minced oath
17. Final
18. Peruses
19. Valley
20. Original work
22. Shops
24. Male offspring
25. Fishing rod and __
26. Speeding
29. Make unfit
33. Elude
34. Factions
35. Convent resident
36. Title
37. Sedate
38. Liquid measure
39. Expire
40. Listened to
41. Over-fond one
42. Careless
44. Unorthodox opinion
45. Spoken
46. Frequently
47. Good luck animal
50. 5-sided figure
55. Operatic solo
56. Martini additive
58. Sonny
59. Prison room
60. Yard brooms
61. Crazy (sl.)
62. Consumes
63. Used money
64. Paradise

DOWN

1. Powder
2. Having wings
3. Organ of smell
4. Shelve (2 wds.)
5. Being concerned
6. Margarine
7. 2-colored horse
8. Conjunction
9. Decreased
10. Uprising
11. Edible seaweed
12. Story
13. Fruit beverages
21. Musical sound
23. English beverages
25. Remodelled

26. Tears
27. Benefit
28. Carved gem
29. Daily record
30. Join together
31. Mysterious letters
32. Doorway
34. Play for time
37. Congressmen
38. Movable
40. Main character
41. Adroit

43. Sung songs
44. Truthful
47. Metal club
48. Region
49. Sediment
50. Tailgate
51. Smooth
52. Virtuous
53. A single time
54. Midday
57. Lick up

PUZZLE 2

ACROSS

1. Examine hastily
5. Marry again
10. Scheme
14. Ripped
15. Irregular
16. Part in play
17. Aardvarks and others
19. Exclude
20. Aye
21. Pass tongue over
22. Made untidy
23. Sweet wine
24. Large bundle
25. Describe exactly
28. Kinsman
32. Got up
33. Gelatinous food
34. Actress Farrow
35. Actress Turner
36. Closes tightly
37. Chums
38. Superlative suffix
39. Form
40. Military call instrument
41. Court meetings
43. Revoke
44. Old Roman March 15
45. Employer
46. Stable compartments
49. Contest
50. Soviet military jet
53. Divide in two
54. One of same graduating group
56. Gaelic
57. Dwelling place
58. May it be so!
59. Hinged opening
60. Verse writers
61. Subdue

DOWN

1. Postpone
2. Ice cream holder
3. Creative works
4. Whose maiden name was
5. Go to bed
6. Upright
7. Labor
8. Curvy letter
9. "Cyrano __ Bergerac"
10. Adjust beforehand
11. Throws in high curve
12. Winglike structures
13. Dull person (sl.)
18. By oneself
19. Postpone
22. Enclosed shopping centers
23. Leaning Tower of __
24. Pretty woman
25. Valleys

26. Wipe out
27. Baptismal bowls
28. Cuts grain
29. Likeness
30. Large country house
31. Artist's picture support
33. Denim trousers
36. Oxfords, for example
37. Young dogs
39. Move sideways
40. Out does
42. Precious metal

43. Stirs up
45. Brag
46. Storage building
47. Plant source of poi
48. Likewise
49. Depressed
50. Mother
51. Article
52. Actor Hackman
54. Bill and __
55. Floor covering
57. Horsepower (abbr.)

PUZZLE 3

ACROSS

1. Articles for sale
5. Foundations
10. Phoney
14. Regular
15. Go-between
16. Yoke part
17. Transmit
18. Rent contract
19. Map abbrs.
20. Woes
22. Foreigners
24. Antique auto
25. Paradise
26. Dash
29. Taking beverage
33. Go to press
34. Penalties
35. German "the"
36. Ladder step
37. Rituals
38. Actor Richard __
39. Also
40. Parakeets, for short
41. Hunger for
42. Simple answers (3 wds.)
44. Curled tightly
45. Necessity
46. Concealed

47. Swellings
50. Shocking events
55. Aloud
56. Particles
58. Hawaiian feast
59. Monster
60. Feel blindly for
61. Famous canal
62. Shades of crimson
63. More recent
64. Beach stuff

DOWN

1. Direction of sunset
2. Declare
3. Nevada city
4. Lasting
5. Vote
6. American writer
7. Oceans
8. Type measures
9. Makes stable
10. Dwindle
11. Detest
12. So be it
13. Shambles
21. Folded
23. Camera part
25. Sea eagles

26. Thick mist
27. Dried plum
28. Citrus skins, e.g.
29. Repeat (colloq.)
30. Perfect
31. Boldness
32. Avarice
34. Devil
37. Plan again
38. Frying pans
40. Leg joint
41. Dime, e.g.

43. Fishes
44. Pursuer
47. Rude person
48. Insist
49. Animal fat
50. Put away
51. ___ Cod
52. Halo
53. Reclined
54. Took to court
57. Mineral

PUZZLE 4

ACROSS

1. Red light
5. Gift to husband
10. Steals
14. __ Turner; actress
15. Angry
16. Taj Mahal site
17. Monkeys
18. Mercenary
19. Banner
20. Most disorderly
22. Worn-out
24. Tax agency (abbr.)
25. Wood fastener
26. On the water
29. Promoted
33. Presses
34. Rhythm and __ music
35. Epoch
36. Uses a straw
37. Solid
38. Wood strip
39. Gen. Robert E. __
40. Short jackets
41. Unpleasant sound
42. Attempting
44. Hovering vehicle
45. Soccer star
46. Chance

47. Pass by
50. Honey sources
55. Factory
56. Swap
58. Roof edge
59. Small land mass
60. Stories
61. Dagger
62. Light beams
63. Suppose
64. Take care of

DOWN

1. Strike
2. Recording
3. Singles
4. Strong feelings
5. Strip
6. Raw metals
7. Desire
8. Arrival time (abbr.)
9. Let go of
10. Lottery
11. Make eyes at
12. Unruly child
13. Wise
21. Retirement accounts (abbr.)
23. Is the right size

25. Object words
26. Walkway
27. Sautes
28. Runs loosely
29. Threw
30. Set afire again
31. Rub out
32. Time reckoner
34. Daniel __; pioneer
37. Small dagger
38. Wettest
40. Organs of sight

41. Ark builder
43. Cider fruits
44. Parmesan or cheddar
47. Arabian prince
48. Mona __
49. Partner
50. Indonesian island
51. Paradise
52. Weathercock
53. Smooth
54. Plant grass
57. Knock

PUZZLE 5

ACROSS

1. Short time periods (abbr.)
5. Staff of life
10. Soaks flax
14. Wheel rod
15. Fraternity hall
16. Wicked
17. Praise
18. Thing of value
19. Vision or phone (prefix)
20. Preserves in chemicals
22. Deserved
24. Man's dinner attire; black ___
25. Big
27. Assistants
30. Sun (Lat.)
31. Desert watering place
35. Lyric poem
36. Emotional shock
39. Type of fish
40. Johnny ___; soldier
41. Girl's nickname
42. Eyeball (poet.)
44. Girl (sl.)
45. Animal appendage
47. Seasickness
49. Colony insect
50. Change
52. Summer time (abbr.)
53. Worries
55. Farm fowls

57. Type of fish
58. Fleet of warships
61. Ancient time piece
65. Refrigerate
66. Wanderer
69. Ore vein
70. False god
71. Court case
72. Female sheep
73. Disclaim
74. Shoe parts
75. Impudent speech

DOWN

1. Transfer property
2. Test
3. Caveman's weapon
4. Make calm
5. Accuse
6. Betsy ___
7. Belonging to the talking horse
8. Era
9. Discourage
10. Secluded place
11. Tied
12. Floor or wall covering
13. Snow vehicle
21. Rosters
23. Past
25. Bud Abbott and ___ Costello
26. Very nearly

27. Main artery
28. Perfect
29. Accountant's entry
30. Restaurant bar creations
32. Sweetener
33. Silly
34. Adds seasoning
37. Raced
38. Exist
43. Breakfast meat
46. Lawfully
48. Employ
51. __, white and blue

54. Confuses
56. Our planet
57. Ringlets
58. Tart; sour
59. Went by horse
60. Night light
61. Close an envelope
62. Hawkeye State
63. Summer drinks
64. Minus
67. Mine find
68. Contend

PUZZLE 6

ACROSS

1. Dull person
5. Used mucilage
10. Uses oars
14. Fury
15. Rope with a noose for catching livestock
16. Wicked
17. Lubricates
18. Be flexible
19. Be concerned
20. Make ready
22. Followed
24. Poem
25. Lovers' meeting
27. Snapshot
30. Tiny
31. Retains
35. Tie fabric
36. Easter __
39. Cut quickly
40. Anger
41. Neckwear
42. Ocean
44. New Deal agency (abbr.)
45. Additional
47. Toils
49. Age
50. Perform
52. Formal wear, for short
53. Portions
55. Vows
57. Help
58. Comings and __
61. Moving slowly
65. Singing voice
66. Amid
69. Silkworm
70. Thailand, formerly
71. Extent
72. Tumble
73. Sanctified
74. Guide
75. Directions (init.)

DOWN

1. Short riding whip
2. Den
3. Leer
4. Tyrant
5. Harsh light
6. Scoop
7. America
8. Special sense
9. Dorothy's nickname
10. Recounts
11. Egg-shaped
12. Metal strand
13. Snow vehicle
21. Take as one's own
23. Inquire
25. Beverage

25. Beverage
26. Boston team
27. Very choice
28. Wading bird
29. Music drama
30. Circle of leaves
32. Come in
33. Turn
34. Crosses
37. Trouble
38. Ever (poet.)
43. Jellied dish
46. Thrift
48. Transport vehicle

51. Label
54. Stick
56. Russian rulers
57. Wrath
58. Deep cut
59. Mixture
60. Type style (abbr.)
61. Playwright
62. Raw steel
63. River in Egypt
64. "Buffalo __"
67. Floor covering
68. Singleton

PUZZLE 7

ACROSS

1. Money accumulated or paid
5. Blackboard
10. __ la la
13. California city
14. Large rabbits
15. Drink
16. English river
17. Portents
18. Heap
19. Business combinations
21. Harms
23. Abraham's nephew
24. Entrance hall
25. Loaded
28. Merriment
29. Pester
33. Greek god of war
34. Deep hole
35. Oar
36. 1st workday (abbr.)
37. Unaffected
39. Beetle
40. Of the stars
42. Paddle a boat
43. Abominable Snowman
44. Bowling alley button
45. Scarlet
46. Not as good
47. Spouses
49. __ Costello
50. Verbally abuses
53. Flags
57. Chief Norse god
58. Cube puzzle inventor
60. Increase
61. Twist
62. Quench
63. __ Fitzgerald
64. Direction (abbr.)
65. Anesthetic
66. Depend

DOWN

1. Heavy jarring impact
2. Small bay
3. Scent
4. Prickling sensations
5. Brief
6. Runs away (sl.)
7. Exist
8. Muscle fiber
9. Treatise
10. Small branch
11. Make angry
12. Grows older
15. Left unhurt
20. Long time
22. Tin or iron
24. Times to come

25. Truman's birthplace
26. Got up
27. Fender mishaps
28. Suitable
30. Poisonous snake
31. Narrow openings
32. Weird
34. Buddy
35. Animal foot
37. Of birth
38. Fishing pole
41. Jog the memory
43. Less mature

45. End product
46. Was victorious
48. Succinct
49. L.A. basketball player
50. Housecoat
51. Adam's garden
52. Ivy plant
53. 2-wheeled vehicle
54. __ Stanley Gardner; author
55. Dinner bread
56. Move to and fro
59. Humbug

1	2	3	4	■	5	6	7	8	9	■	■	10	11	12
13				■	14					■	15			
16				■	17					■	18			
19				20			■	21		22				
■	■	■	23			■	24				■	■	■	■
25	26	27			■	28			■	29		30	31	32
33				■	34			■	35					
36			■	37			■	38			■	39		
40			41			■	42			■	43			
44				■	45			■	46					
■	■	■	47		48			■	49			■	■	■
50	51	52				■	53			■	54	55	56	
57				■	58		59			■	60			
61				■	62				■	■	63			
64				■	65					■	66			

PUZZLE 8

ACROSS

1. Seaweed
5. Frog's cousin
9. Persian poet
13. Oceans
14. Dig out
15. Ripped
16. Turn-of-the-century footwear
19. Curly letter
20. Inlets
21. Writing tools
22. Fish "lung"
23. Bad smell
25. Aid
28. Elevated
31. Unadorned
32. Path
34. Among (poet.)
36. Slay
37. Meal plans
38. Actor Richard __
39. Theater sign
40. Unguent
41. Sudden rush
42. Something to bless
44. __ella
45. Untruths
46. Young bears
47. "The Wizard __"
49. Deciding panel
50. Kind or sort
53. Protective garment (2 wds.)
57. American indian
58. Walkway
59. Sound quality
60. Electrical units
61. Wagers
62. Again

DOWN

1. Arthur __ ,tennis champ
2. Flower wreaths
3. Fast jokes
4. Fine cinders
5. Sum
6. Ins and __
7. Past
8. Cozy room
9. Different ones
10. Night light
11. War god
12. Musical notes
14. Culpability
17. Bracing
18. Go bad
22. Lass
23. Speechify
24. Platform

25. Inquires
26. Agitates
27. Beauty shop
29. Correct
30. Funeral song
32. Ceramic squares
33. Race engine
35. Horned animal
37. Stupor
38. Weapons
40. Take by force
41. Mid-east nation
43. Runs away

44. Malediction
46. Ringlets
47. Vow
48. Out of
49. Joke
50. Raw steel
51. Solitary
52. Had information
53. Dove sound
54. Catch or arrest
55. Neckwear
56. School group

1	2	3	4			5	6	7	8		9	10	11	12
13					14						15			
16				17						18				
19					20						21			
			22						23	24				
25	26	27					28					29	30	
31						32	33					34		35
36				37							38			
39				40					41					
	42		43					44						
		45				46								
	47	48				49					50	51	52	
53				54	55				56					
57				58					59					
60				61					62					

PUZZLE 9

ACROSS

1. Flat floating platform
5. Braid
10. Clothed
14. Beige
15. Spear
16. Parasites
17. Antlered animal
18. Star-like flower
19. English queen
20. Large flightless bird
22. Chanced
24. Sooner
25. Toothed wheels
27. __ Claus
30. Jinx
31. Retains
35. Bull ring cheer
36. Worked
39. Small arrow
40. Fish eggs
41. Epoch
42. Regret
44. Take to court
45. Ceases
47. Declared
49. Direction (abbr.)
50. Relaxes
52. __ and downs
53. Did nothing
55. Lift
57. Rural address abbreviation
58. Leather strips
61. Busies oneself
65. Persia
66. Tasty
69. Top-notch (comp. wd.)
70. Discover
71. Join
72. Press
73. Toddlers
74. Ardent
75. Bird's home

DOWN

1. Do again
2. High cards
3. Worry
4. Small tower
5. Location
6. Eyelid hair
7. Picnic pest
8. Frost
9. Earth
10. Categorized
11. Chain part
12. Skin problem
13. Land title
21. Angry
23. Annoy
25. Set
26. Strives

27. More painful
28. Solitary
29. Requires
30. Interruption
32. Artist's stand
33. Dried plum
34. Horse
37. Eithers
38. Payable
43. Prepares copy
46. Strings
48. Monkey
51. Tree fluid

54. Keep back
56. Edition
57. More impolite
58. Sieve
59. Threesome
60. Rave
61. Sink teeth into
62. Traditional knowledge
63. Adam's grandson
64. Transmitted
67. Collection
68. Swine

PUZZLE 10

ACROSS

1. Narcotic
5. Word plays
9. Other
13. Declare
14. Fabric print method
15. Lend
16. Wedding permit (2 wds.)
19. Large deer kin
20. Makes a knot
21. Streets (abbr.)
22. Fuse metal
23. Leisurely run
25. Animal emblems
28. Happenings
31. Iridescent gems
32. Cut off
34. Consume
36. Plow
37. Say
38. Strong wind
39. Yoko ___
40. Small sign
41. Fire crime
42. Pep
44. Pal
45. Prevaricates
46. Hurried
47. ___ Guinness

49. Work for
50. School organization (abbr.)
53. Halloween visitors (comp. wd.)
57. Cleft
58. Entrances
59. On
60. "Beware the ___ of March"
61. Disavow
62. Obtains

DOWN

1. Woman of rank
2. Ellipse
3. Make coffee
4. Make a mistake
5. Summoned
6. Western Indians
7. Nothing
8. Glide on snow
9. 1st 2-digit prime
10. Solitary
11. Back talk
12. Direction (abbr.)
14. Scoops out
17. News bits
18. Frolic
22. Water source
23. Embankment
24. Above

25. Dorothy's dog
26. Suppose
27. Bird's claw
29. Pester
30. Beauty parlor
32. Remains
33. And so on (abbr.)
35. Take care of
37. Whim
38. Grill
40. Prank
41. Battlefield
43. Votes into office

44. Flames
46. Torment
47. Dry
48. Animation
49. English college
50. __ Rose; baseball player
51. Brisk pace
52. Snakes
53. Three (pref.)
54. Strange
55. Fish eggs
56. Label

PUZZLE 11

ACROSS

1. "__ the night before Christmas, . . ."
5. Hit hard
10. __ Huntley
14. Robust
15. Water walker
16. Rabbit
17. On the ocean
18. Pointless
19. __ Lanchester
20. Healing treatment
22. Moon impression
24. Adam's mate
25. Costume (colloq.)
27. Slip
30. Wind instrument
31. Blur
35. Out of sight
36. Varied between limits
39. Men's charitable organization
40. Lincoln
41. Ascot
42. WWII Russian fighter plane
44. Cup
45. Men's college group
47. Moisten
49. Devoured
50. Stories
52. Tool assembly
53. Donkeys
55. Lock of hair
57. Brother (sl.)
58. Moor
61. Food fish
65. Flame
66. Grader
69. __ Horne
70. Winged
71. Sea
72. Dines
73. Yanks counterpart
74. Tall grass
75. Groups of two

DOWN

1. The one farther away
2. Bathe
3. Toward the sheltered side
4. Scorched
5. Pilfer (sl.)
6. Numerous
7. __ Lupino
8. Tithing percent
9. Build
10. Inexpensively
11. Cease
12. Gaelic
13. Weep drop
21. Avoid
23. Polish
25. Joke

26. Nontaxable
27. Cheat someone (sl.)
28. Astrological sign
29. Aim
30. Prowls
32. __ Samms, et al.
33. Critical
34. Spells of fury
37. Assist
38. Expire
43. Twist
46. Restrains
48. Wrong (pref.)

51. Theater sign
54. Dirty
56. Mistake
57. Stables
58. From a distance
59. Egyptian river
60. Shellfish
61. Skull location
62. Male friend
63. To (Bib.)
64. Russian news service
67. Expert
68. Golf peg

1	2	3	4		5	6	7	8	9		10	11	12	13
14					15						16			
17					18						19			
20				21					22	23				
			24				25	26						
27	28	29				30				31		32	33	34
35				36	37			38		39				
40				41				42		43		44		
45			46		47		48					49		
50			51		52				53	54				
		55		56				57						
58	59	60					61				62	63	64	
65				66	67	68				69				
70				71						72				
73				74						75				

PUZZLE 12

ACROSS

1. Wise or prudent
5. Carbonated beverage
9. Some (2 wds.)
13. Eye flirtingly
14. Funny
15. Heroic narrative
16. Time (2 wds.)
19. Mature
20. Plant feeder
21. Compressed air
22. Hurt
23. Electrical units
25. Open __, magic words
28. __ with, encounter (2 wds.)
31. Mass
32. Trample
34. Doze
36. Lyric poems
37. Beat
38. First king of Israel
39. Marry
40. Enjoys
41. Upper part of body
42. Directions for cooking
44. Frothed
45. Prayer ending
46. Complete failure (colloq.)
47. Door frame
49. Impudent child
50. Large body of water
53. Interval with nothing to do (4 wds.)
57. Sin
58. Strange
59. Exclamation of disgust
60. Koppel, et al.
61. Desire
62. Comply

DOWN

1. Wide padded seat
2. Full of surprise
3. Adhesive
4. Ever (poet.)
5. __ and Gomorrah
6. Leave out
7. Not bright
8. Expert
9. Aid
10. Festival
11. Inner selves
12. Pallid
14. Task
17. Vagrant
18. Titled
22. Pork cuts
23. Signs of the future
24. Command
25. Barge

26. Church leader
27. Napped leather
29. Take away a weapon
30. Rest
32. Sign
33. Be sorry for
35. Trudge
37. Water line
38. Cleansing agent
40. Indeterminate state
41. Mouth part
43. Humped animals

44. Outburst of flame
46. Apple, for one
47. Insincere talk (sl.)
48. Among
49. Out of womb
50. Ignore
51. Rim
52. Sooty
53. Vietnam offensive
54. Unused
55. Affirmative vote
56. Military address (abbr.

PUZZLE 13

ACROSS

1. Mimic
5. Wool producer
10. Marquis de __
14. Man or boy
15. Go
16. Cat sound
17. Spheres
18. Made less rigid
19. Seep
20. Restraining device (2 wds.)
22. Presser
24. Pouring edge
25. Native of Glasgow
26. Tailed heavenly bodies
29. __ comfort
33. Gather together
34. Extra
35. Sheltered side
36. Catches
37. Akin
38. Girl (sl.)
39. He and ___
40. Leg joints
41. Deprived of, as breath
42. Skilled
44. Innocently
45. Cast off, as a lover
46. Garden tool
47. Erase
50. Do __ (kill -2 wds.)
55. Administrative officer (colloq.)
56. Rants
58. Thought
59. Cloth fuzz
60. Run away to marry
61. Remainder
62. Airline info (pl.)
63. Impressions
64. Italian family name

DOWN

1. __ and Andy
2. Peel
3. Island of exile
4. Unsettled
5. Takes 40 winks
6. Cure
7. The Orient
8. Adam's wife
9. Foot care
10. Without bumps
11. Long time
12. Nod off
13. Jug
21. Pieces
23. Repetition
25. Saturates

26. Am able (Bib.)
27. City in Nebraska
28. "Black Label" waitress
29. Watched
30. Make happy
31. One who revolts
32. The poor
34. Frozen rain
37. Horned
38. Exposed electrical cord (2 wds.)
40. Loop yarn
41. Float

43. Ousts
44. Stages of development
47. Remove from print
48. Leave
49. __ Horne
50. Bard's river
51. Cried
52. __ of March
53. Try
54. Detest
57. Fermented beverage

PUZZLE 14

ACROSS

1. Large sea mammal
5. Skillful
10. Snow vehicle
14. Factual
15. Zest
16. Soccer star
17. Melodies
18. Perfect
19. Demolish
20. Explanations
22. Idler
24. Unit of work
25. Ore evaluation
27. Sports center
30. Insecticide
31. Lukewarm
35. Conflict
36. Theme paper
39. Finished
40. Beverage
41. Time period
42. Gun group (init.)
44. Military service (abbr.)
45. Wealthy
47. Small drums
49. Musical notes
50. Was overly fond
52. Plaything
53. Sample
55. Bore
57. Wager
58. Hand gun
61. Soils
65. Author Philip __
66. Expect
69. Resentful appreciation
70. American Indian
71. Shoe bottoms
72. ___ gun
73. Daybreak
74. Shabby
75. Ripped

DOWN

1. Play the leading role
2. Pennsylvania city
3. Halo
4. Diminish
5. Maturing
6. Failures
7. Wind direction (init.)
8. School meeting
9. Highway fees
10. Used aerosol
11. Foliage
12. Otherwise
13. Horned animal
21. Make a speech
23. Cereal grain
25. Commercials, for short
26. Miserly

27. Grant
28. Sound receiver
29. Upright
30. Indicate
32. Rains hard
33. Map enhancement
34. Thick
37. Word with nail or nob
38. Theater sign
43. Fall flower
46. Godless one
48. And not
51. Twosome

54. Testify
56. Window pane
57. Itsy __
58. Goad
59. Particle
60. Put away
61. Expired
62. Within
63. Always
64. Auld Lang __
67. Misery
68. Dark beer

1	2	3	4		5	6	7	8	9		10	11	12	13
14					15						16			
17					18						19			
20				21					22	23				
			24				25	26						
27	28	29				30				31		32	33	34
35				36	37				38		39			
40				41			42		43		44			
45			46		47		48					49		
50				51		52			53	54				
			55		56			57						
58	59	60					61				62	63	64	
65				66	67	68			69					
70				71					72					
73				74					75					

PUZZLE 15

ACROSS

1. Clothing
5. Type of metal
10. Seize (colloq.)
13. Medicinal plant
14. Noon meal
15. The good guy
16. Dinner, e.g.
17. Result from
18. Dines
19. Most uncanny
21. Discounts
23. Printer's measures
24. Mistake
25. Living
28. Compensate
29. Fire residue
33. Type of citrus
34. Disfigure
35. Chicken piece
36. __ Gabor; actress
37. Copper coins
39. Social insurance
   group (abbr.)
40. Area
42. Terminate
43. Leading actor
44. Lock of hair
45. Inquire
46. An eye for __ (2 wds.)
47. Smallest amount

49. Falsehood
50. Marches
53. Cautious
57. Prayer ending
58. Manlike machine
60. City district
61. __ Piper
62. Angry
63. Famous canal
64. Find the sum
65. Anesthetic
66. Matched groups

DOWN

1. Playing activity
2. To the sheltered side
3. Lion sound
4. Have faith
5. "God __ America"
6. Smallest of litter
7. Reply (abbr.)
8. Go hastily
9. Very steep
10. Tidy
11. __ Johnson; comedian
12. Employer
15. Funeral car
20. Wind direction (abbr.)
22. Wild hogs
24. Sincere
25. Wide awake

26. Menu item; __ and onions
27. Mirror reflection
28. Cooking vessel
30. "__ makes waste"
31. Type of composition
32. Gaze steadily
34. Males
35. Sleeping place
37. Modeled
38. Writing fluid
41. Land surrounded by water
43. Cold symptoms

45. Separate into classes
46. Ventilate
48. Eagle's nest
49. After awhile
50. Mama and __
51. In the middle of
52. Type of grass
53. Pigeon shelter
54. Golfer's cry
55. One
56. Dregs
59. Exclamation of disgust

PUZZLE 16

ACROSS

1. Wound cover
5. Precise times
10. Russian ruler
14. Halo
15. Outcast
16. Regarding (2 wds.)
17. Actor ___ Morris
18. Citrus
19. Diplomacy
20. Metal fastener
22. Tombstone writings
24. Particle
26. Spirit
27. Book sections
31. Urge
35. Lassos
36. Spars
38. Enlisted officer
39. Baseball officials (abbr.)
40. Wheeled platform
41. Extend across
42. Singer Torme
43. Attend
44. Accustom
45. Ruptures
47. Controls
49. Uses ladle
51. Jog
52. Nice
56. Ship's weight
60. Lighting device
61. Aquatic mammals
63. Bee home
64. Mine entrance
65. Strange
66. Paradise
67. N.Y. hoop team
68. Laundromat feature
69. Impression

DOWN

1. Droops
2. Actor ___ Jurgens
3. Neighborhood
4. Scots wind instruments
5. Take out
6. Cutting tool
7. Use a stopwatch
8. Run away
9. Old age problem
10. Giants
11. Small cookie
12. Curbed portal
13. Soaks
21. Land parcels
23. Sun-bathes
25. Knight's wear

27. Bread particle
28. Baseball event
29. Fall fruit
30. Round of gunfire
32. Information given
33. Frighten
34. Vocal qualities
37. Slumbered
40. Hated
41. Grabbed
43. Snow runners
44. Press

46. Is flexible
48. Pencil end
50. Show derision
52. Scheme
53. Freight
54. Give off
55. A Crosby
57. Conceal
58. Kiln
59. Hire
62. Recline

1	2	3	4		5	6	7	8	9		10	11	12	13
14					15						16			
17					18						19			
20				21			22			23				
			24			25		26						
27	28	29					30		31			32	33	34
35						36		37				38		
39					40						41			
42				43						44				
45			46				47		48					
			49			50		51						
52	53	54				55		56			57	58	59	
60					61			62			63			
64					65						66			
67					68						69			

PUZZLE 17

ACROSS

1. Coming after proper time
5. Conductor's stick
10. Most excellent
14. Portent
15. Cognizant
16. Great Lake
17. Reclining
18. Loans
19. Angle function
20. Best
22. Table places
24. Sour substance
26. Peruse
27. Earth shelves
31. Lubricate
35. Foreign
36. Sudden pains
38. __ Diego
39. Gentle
40. Business symbols
41. Potato
42. Summer (Fr.)
43. Sinks teeth into
44. Portion
45. Tyrant
47. Came back
49. Pro __; proportionately
51. Trade for money
52. Formal arguers
56. Slanted
60. Leave out
61. Perch
63. Jot
64. Embankment
65. Show feeling
66. Standard
67. Raw metals
68. Person one goes out with
69. Females

DOWN

1. Waste time
2. Both (pref.)
3. Adolescent
4. Made more beloved
5. Scandinavian sea
6. Wonder
7. Makes leather
8. Command
9. Savings accounts (2 wds
10. Next to
11. Ireland
12. Vocalize a melody
13. Golf ball holders
21. Read quickly
23. __ and feathers
25. Train station

25. Dull pain
26. Participate in
27. Emergency sound
29. Trivial
30. Hoarded
32. Charged as penalty
33. Lower limb
35. That woman's
37. Bull (Sp.)
38. Taunt
40. Enticed
41. Theater piece
43. Backbones

44. Alcohol (sl.)
46. Wall steps
47. Short jacket
48. Pace
49. Calculates
50. Another name for Ireland
51. Agitate
52. Insect
53. Theater sign
54. Tree
55. ___ Grande
56. Marker

1	2	3	4			5	6	7	8			9	10	11	12
13					14							15			
16				17						18					
19				20						21					
			22					23	24						
25	26	27					28				29	30			
31					32	33				34			35		
36				37					38						
39			40					41							
	42	43					44								
		45				46									
	47	48				49					50	51	52		
53				54	55				56						
57				58					59						
60				61					62						

PUZZLE 19

ACROSS

1. Savory plant
5. Castle ditches
10. Sign
14. To the sheltered side
15. Luxury boat
16. Storm
17. Hope __; actress
18. Guide
19. Work units
20. As scheduled (2 wds.)
22. Least
24. Nothing (pl.)
26. Adam's grandson
27. Relocate
31. Oil
35. Belonging to Nathan
36. Adored
38. Moving truck
39. Aroma
40. Knack
41. Hairless
42. Texas border river;
    __ Grande
43. Out of date (Fr.)
44. Living
45. Childish protest (2 wds.)
47. Toured
49. Bristle

51. Whirl
52. Photograph
56. Confused
60. Possess
61. Upright
63. Uncanny
64. Prayer ending
65. Hidden loot
66. Chest sound
67. Disorder
68. Good to eat
69. Raced

DOWN

1. Angel's hat
2. Ardor
3. Lease
4. Novice
5. Me
6. Cereal grain
7. High cards
8. Topic
9. Unfamiliar one
10. Otherwise (2 wds.)
11. Female horse
12. Ova
13. Savings; __ egg
21. Fail to hit
23. Master

PUZZLE 29

25. Vends

27. Rose sticker

28. Music box

29. Reserved; cool

30. Cut of meat

32. Make accessible

33. Ointment

34. Finished

37. Contenders

40. Most distant

41. Mixers

43. Large tarts

44. Eager

46. Colorado trees

48. Disinterest

50. Main artery

52. Imitation

53. Title

54. Streets (abbr.)

55. Afternoon parties

57. Jump

58. __ Stanley Gardner

59. Tinted

62. Time zone (abbr.)

1	2	3	4	■	5	6	7	8	9	■	10	11	12	13
14					15						16			
17					18						19			
20				21		■	22			23				
■	■		24			25		26				■	■	■
27	28	29					30		31			32	33	34
35						36		37			■	38		
39				■	40					■	41			
42			■	43					■	44				
45			46			■	47		48					
■	■	49			50	■	51				■	■	■	■
52	53	54				55	■	56			57	58	59	
60			■	61			62		■	63				
64			■	65				■	66					
67				■	68			■	69					

PUZZLE 20

ACROSS

1. Laughter
5. Isle of __
10. Sound of thunder
14. Above
15. Assumed name
16. Fairy tale monster
17. Usual state
19. Bargain events
20. Female sheep
21. Antlered animals
22. Beat out grain
23. Words of understanding (2 wds.)
24. Grating
25. Dread
28. Do business
32. Pry
33. Braces
34. Remunerate
35. Business abbreviation
36. Attracts
37. Angel's instrument
38. Regret
39. Destines to tragedy
40. Arc
41. Meetings
43. Moistens the roast
44. Rabbit
45. Gala event (sl.)
46. Candles
49. Kind
50. Certified Public Accountant (abbr.)
53. Orderly grouping
54. Beginning point
56. Sidelong look
57. Mean
58. Healing plant
59. Girl
60. __ Adams, columnist
61. N.Y. ball club

DOWN

1. Sharpen
2. Declare openly
3. This place
4. Appendage
5. Page
6. Similar
7. Holes
8. Beam
9. Exists
10. Planks
11. Make eyes at
12. Crude metals
13. Net
18. Fable writer
19. Shanks
22. Snares
23. Press
24. Enlarges

25. Russian rulers
26. Follow
27. Lover's flowers
28. Streetcars
29. Separated
30. Etch
31. Varieties
33. Inclined
36. Entrance
37. Quiet
39. Daily log
40. Flings
42. Scissors

43. Merely
45. Tire with dullness
46. High
47. Region
48. Chief executive (abbr.)
49. Avoid
50. Nat King __
51. Scheme
52. Summer coolers
54. Three (comb.)
55. Pork product
57. Syringe abbreviation

PUZZLE 21

ACROSS

1. Warehouse upper floor
5. Tableland
9. New York baseball team
13. Operatic solo
14. Challenges
15. Prepare for publication
16. Interest paid (2 wds.)
19. Hardwood tree
20. The selves
21. Falsehoods
22. Bristle
23. Jogging gait
25. Give account of
28. Removed soap
31. Works for
32. Tenant's contract
34. Large tank
36. Excited
37. Grimace
38. Nevada city
39. Lair
40. Metal fastener
41. Rudolph's master
42. Rest
44. Separated
45. Singer Ed __
46. Bundle of hay
47. Golf cry
49. Male parent (animals)
50. Automobile
53. Football term (3 wds.)
57. Baking stove
58. Readies for shipment
59. Expression of approval
60. Sunset direction
61. Colony insects
62. Bird's home

DOWN

1. Fine net
2. Verbal
3. Unyielding
4. Sticky substance
5. Feudal estate
6. Units of work
7. Minute part (abbr.)
8. Hardwood tree
9. Deserves
10. Border
11. Binds
12. City roads (abbr.)
14. Numeral from 0 to 9
17. Decade parts
18. By one's self
22. __ Kong
23. Piece of land
24. Ascend

25. Observe writing
26. Anxious
27. Lying flat
29. A happening
30. "Divine Comedy" author
32. Continues to exist
33. Compass pt. (abbr.)
35. Warty frog
37. Having wisdom
38. Scarce
40. Juliet's lover
41. Oregon capital
43. Father or mother

44. French capital
46. Feathered friends
47. Cents in a nickel
48. Dollar bills
49. Go away, cat
50. Made an appearance
51. Matures
52. Tenant's payment
53. Of little height
54. Sunshine State (abbr.)
55. Tater to Snuffy
56. Adult male

PUZZLE 22

ACROSS

1. Rash and foolish
4. Baseball hat
7. Electrical current (abbr.)
10. Landed
12. Artist's subject
14. Merriment
15. Lion sound
16. Silly
17. Cruising
18. Chooses
20. Rabbit's treat
22. Edible seed
23. Feasted
24. Secret symbols
26. Grease
27. Flesh
30. Charts
31. Sack
32. Door hangers
34. Poem
35. Gathering of people
37. Picnic pest
38. Dot
40. Anger
41. Large town
42. Chore
43. Consumed
44. Male heirs
45. Suspicious

47. Household animal
48. Complainer
50. Tell secrets
53. Cent
54. Topical
56. Mistake sound
58. Small lake
59. Group of bees
60. Christmas carol
61. Inquire
62. Depot (abbr.)
63. Lock opener

DOWN

1. Damage
2. Medicinal plant
3. Clock face
4. Pros and __
5. Oklahoma town
6. Writing stick
7. And; plus
8. Encounter
9. Pod vegetable
11. Fashions
12. Baseball glove
13. Jack Sprat's meat
14. Flower or vegetable __
19. Pool stick
21. Send payment
23. Self-respect

24. Officer trainee
25. Musical drama
26. Boat paddle
28. Once more
29. Camper's homes
30. Scrub the floor
31. Unopened flower
32. Color; tint
33. Pigpen
35. Symbol
36. Mine find
39. Land surrounded by water
41. Type of material

43. Bows and ___
44. Matched pieces
46. Long fishes
47. Tropical tree
48. Cow sounds
49. Hog sound
50. Scarlet O'Hara's home
51. See
52. Fencing sword
53. Accountant (abbr.)
55. Feline
57. Crafty

PUZZLE 23

ACROSS

1. Couch
5. Artificial bird
10. Joke
14. So it is!
15. Leave out
16. __ Mountains of USSR
17. Circulate fresh air
19. Flash off and on
20. N and n
21. Attractive
22. Golden Gate structure
23. Current fashion
24. Mystery-solving fact
25. Purify
28. Waves
32. In wrong way
33. Curving outward
34. Rodent
35. Young male horse
36. Froths
37. Set of signals
38. Summer (Fr.)
39. Harbors
40. Term of address for lady
41. Sweet courses
43. Overlays
44. Flat receptacle
45. Companion
46. Oily
49. Walking stick
50. Devoured
53. Actor Greene
54. Finished
56. Greedy
57. Largest of deer
58. Orange-red stone
59. Lairs
60. Country bumpkin
61. Television award

DOWN

1. Put aside as a reserve
2. Portent
3. Swamps
4. Colonial insect
5. Mislead
6. Make joyful
7. Summon before court
8. Lyric poem
9. "Oh, Come All __ Faithful"
10. "Romeo and __"
11. Dry and barren
12. Sudden pain
13. Actress Sommer
18. Images
19. Like an animal
22. Smudges
23. Fine spray
24. Shellfish (pl.)

25. Competed in speed contest

26. Act in theatrical way (colloq.)

27. Grinding tools

28. Low-heeled shoes

29. Wear away

30. Detecting device

31. Stalks

33. __ winks; nap (colloq.)

36. Sudden raid

37. Grotto

39. By itself (2 wds.)

40. Hotel for motorists

42. Remains upright

43. Cross out

45. Parsonage

46. __ rags; fine clothes (sl.)

47. Wander

48. Ireland (poet.)

49. Chef

50. First man (Bib.)

51. School year division

52. Little whirlpool

54. Bill and __

55. Utilize

57. Belonging to me

1	2	3	4	■	5	6	7	8	9	■	10	11	12	13
14				■	15					■	16			
17				18					■	19				
20			■	21				■	22					
■	■	23					■	24				■	■	■
25	26	27			■	28				■	29	30	31
32				■	33				■	34			
35			■	36				■	37				
38			■	39				■	40				
41			42				■	43					
■	■	■	44				■	45				■	■	■
46	47	48			■	49				■	50	51	52
53				■	54				■	55			
56				■	57				■	58			
59				■	60				■	61			

PUZZLE 24

ACROSS

1. Clever plan
5. Openwork fabric
9. Fish's breathing organ
13. Swinging stride
14. Mr. (Sp.)
15. Medicinal plant
16. Slot machines (sl., 2 wds.)
19. Lair
20. Breezy
21. Grows old
22. Sly
23. Donated
25. Remove from office
28. Raises spirits of
31. Worship
32. Last
34. By way of
36. Be pleased with
37. Employs
38. Horn sound
39. Frozen water
40. Paying passengers
41. Cleanse of impurities
42. Sings with vibrato
44. Trade
45. Russian no
46. Twisted
47. Peace symbol
49. Frog's relative
50. Witness
53. Excessively
57. Burden
58. Ice cream holders
59. Reduce strain
60. Surpassing all other
61. Water pitcher
62. Thin wire nail

DOWN

1. Walk heavily
2. "The __ Ranger"
3. Not shut
4. Yes
5. Suspicious
6. Singer __ Williams
7. Woody core of corn
8. Historical period
9. Mechanical device
10. Tennis player Nastas
11. Great number (colloc
12. "__ Miserables"
14. Grin
17. Lift up
18. Of sea forces
22. Used as clothing
23. Heredity factors
24. Cry of regret

25. Painter Salvador __

26. Official order

27. Card game

29. Turn outward

30. Trying time

32. Before any others

33. Anger

35. Mimic

37. Healthy

38. Actor __ Lancaster

40. Aviator

41. Chinese bear like animal

43. Put in money for profit

44. Necklace

46. Stupid blunder (sl.)

47. Sand hill

48. Numbered musical work

49. Melody

50. Featured performer

51. "Born Free" lioness

52. Watched

53. Weep aloud

54. Playing card

55. __ and arrow

56. Bird's bill

PUZZLE 25

ACROSS

1. Still or tranquil
5. Desire greatly
10. Ireland
14. Woodwind instrument
15. Person
16. Russian mountain range
17. Shut loudly
18. Representative
19. Classification
20. Male singing voices
22. Snakes
24. Score
26. Polio shot; __ vaccine
27. Completely
31. Closer
35. Liquor (colloq.)
36. Main artery
38. Biblical priest
39. Skeleton part
40. Belonging to singer Paul
41. Farmer's yield
42. Wind direction (abbr.)
43. Concluded
44. Mold
45. Pattern
47. Eavesdropper
49. Midday
51. Spanish cheers
52. Publishes again
56. Morals
60. Against
61. Sister's daughter
63. Graven image
64. Roman date; __ of March
65. Jewelry fastener
66. Decorate again
67. Misplaced
68. Attempt
69. Orient

DOWN

1. Amount paid
2. Skilled
3. Lend
4. Commit to memory
5. Pure
6. Carpet
7. Ed __; band leader
8. Weather devices
9. Contestants
10. Expression of triumph
11. Asian country
12. Rave
13. Type of antlered animals
21. Scarce
23. Legal request
25. Antlered animal

27. Receded
28. Hangman's rope
29. Bell sounds
30. Bumpkin
32. Raced again
33. Flee to wed
34. More mature
37. CB for one
40. Broadcast
41. "Alice in Wonderland" cat
43. Selves
44. Printer's mark

46. Demand
48. Drowsy
50. Sedaka and Diamond
52. Fence top
53. Within (comb.)
54. Residents (suff.)
55. Mediterranean and Baltic
57. Thought
58. Type of fishes
59. Arcade games; __ machines
62. Confederate group (abbr.)

PUZZLE 26

ACROSS

1. Nail with a small head
5. Quote
9. Locating device
14. Breathing sound
15. Bake spot
16. Run away
17. Tennis star __ Lendl
18. Cover the inside
19. Like shoes
20. Jules Verne captain
21. Went ahead
22. Tempos
23. Tangled
25. Caviar
26. Unit of work
27. Belt or girdle
32. Chinese fryer
35. Long for
37. Carried
38. Sheltered side
40. Break violently
42. Repair
43. Searches
45. Type of girder
47. Pigpen
48. Despairing
50. Pole
52. Printer's measures
53. Orator

57. Be present
61. Pigeon sound
62. Style
63. Sensational
64. Alone
65. Opera song
66. Sleep sound
67. Spirit
68. Turned right
69. Western movie
70. Sailors
71. Facile

DOWN

1. Edge
2. Black bird
3. Texas mission
4. Indicate
5. Schools
6. Some college walls
7. Care for
8. Wind direction
9. Regard
10. Healing plant
11. Mete out
12. Mimicked
13. Shades of scarlet
22. Male child
24. Attempt
25. Wash lightly

27. Complains (colloq.)
28. Male cat
29. American Indians
30. Lease
31. Swirl
32. Lave
33. Margarine
34. Retain
36. Wrongly
39. Scrape out
41. Whaling spears
44. Thin
46. One of Three Stooges

49. Finish
51. Injure
53. Of the sun
54. Scene of 50's conflict
55. Singer Adams and others
56. Prepared
57. Additionally
58. Food fish
59. Jog
60. Ireland
61. Soft drink
64. Matched group

1	2	3	4		5	6	7	8		9	10	11	12	13
14					15					16				
17					18					19				
20					21				22					
23				24				25						
			26				27			28	29	30	31	
32	33	34		35		36			37					
38			39		40			41		42				
43				44		45			46		47			
48				49				50		51				
			52				53			54	55	56		
57	58	59	60			61				62				
63					64				65					
66					67				68					
69					70				71					

PUZZLE 27

ACROSS

1. Remove hat
5. Thick piece
9. Stratagem
13. Reclining
14. South American country
15. Actor's part
16. Rough-terrain vehicles (comp. wd., 2 wds.)
19. __ Kennedy
20. Scarlets
21. Singles
22. Pod vegetables
23. Scheme
25. Potential
28. Plenty (2 wds.)
31. Accumulate
32. Snares
34. __ Tin Tin; TV dog
36. Has to
37. Glow
38. Weathercock
39. N.Y. time (abbr.)
40. Musical study
41. Detests
42. Lash holder
44. Penny pinchers
45. Makes public
46. Lose color
47. Trial
49. Yard tool
50. Tiny
53. Businessmen's garb (comp. wd., 2 wds.)
57. Tumble
58. Central
59. Strike openhanded
60. Greek god of war
61. Adam's grandson
62. Partner

DOWN

1. Foolish
2. Woodwind instrument
3. Family fight
4. Depression president (init.)
5. Gets rid of
6. Prevaricates
7. Every
8. Sleeping place
9. Publishes
10. Adore
11. Bull ring cheers
12. Affirmative
14. Defraud
17. Tiny songbirds
18. Tubers
22. Nuisance
23. Jet
24. Leisurely run

25. Crippled
26. Entertain
27. Delicious
29. Lecture
30. Better
32. Falls heavily
33. Free of
35. Loch __ monster
37. Mix up
38. Flower holder
40. Select group
41. Conceals
43. Artist's stands

44. Creator
46. Looks toward
47. Norse thunder god
48. __ Stanley Gardner; author
49. Nevada city
50. Last __ and testament
51. And others (abbr., 2 wds.)
52. Catch sight of
53. __ la la
54. Crusted dessert
55. Hotel
56. America (abbr.)

PUZZLE 28

ACROSS

1. Having wings
5. Unit of medicine
9. Made angry
14. Ration
15. Within
16. Rub out
17. English river
18. __ Laurel; comedian
19. Glue
20. Confined
21. __ and feather
22. Midpoint
23. Rockaby baby in the __
25. Prohibit
26. Beetle
27. Educated
32. Fruit beverage
35. Anesthetic
37. Heater
38. Profound
40. Rescued
42. On the ocean
43. Arabic god
45. Discourage
47. Cease
48. Wrong name
50. Suitable
52. __ Vegas
53. Reminiscences
57. Meal
61. That woman
62. Afresh
63. Take as one's own
64. Speck of dust
65. Certain
66. Nervous
67. Unlock
68. Accurate
69. Mocking smile
70. Saucy
71. Transmitted

DOWN

1. Adjust to conditions
2. Intimate
3. Solitary
4. Leased
5. Twists out of shape
6. Drawn from a cask (2 wds.)
7. Celebrity
8. Long time
9. Feels regret
10. Persia
11. Endure
12. This (Sp.)
13. Antlered animal
22. Feline
24. Foot digit
25. French cap

27. Crowbar
28. Arrival time (abbr.)
29. American Beauty
30. Smooth
31. Inanimate
32. 1st man
33. Food shop
34. Long fishes
36. Underworld
39. Frying tool
41. Submissive
44. Gun holder
46. Brim

49. Pad
51. Makes crisp and brown
53. Length measure
54. Harden
55. Summer TV fare
56. Sugary
57. Rodents
58. Eve's garden
59. Corn bread
60. Church part
61. Wish
64. Wash floors

PUZZLE 29

ACROSS

1. Branch of learning
5. Turns white
10. Lean-to
14. Male sweetheart
15. Wide awake
16. Birthday food
17. Table light
18. Cook stove
19. Type of bird
20. Circus attraction
22. On deck
24. Boy
25. False god
26. Motor
29. Certain oilmen
33. Type of stationery
34. Distributed
35. Wager
36. Actress Arthur and others
37. Containing sodium
38. Indian bread
39. Halloween month (abbr.)
40. Type of bird
41. Gift recipient
42. Cowboy stories
44. Huck Finn's friend; Tom ___
45. Pieces of cloth
46. Resident of (suff.)
47. Word of warning
50. Respected
55. Dry
56. Oak seed
58. Dog's name
59. Existence
60. Hangman's rope
61. One
62. Wine dregs
63. Carried
64. Allows

DOWN

1. Having skill or resources
2. Genuine
3. Domesticated
4. Furnishes
5. Float event
6. Actor; ___ Alda
7. Fasting period
8. Work unit
9. Constantly
10. Roll of writings
11. Laugh sound (hyph.)
12. One who barely gets by
13. Not living
21. Hired helper
23. Place for a nut
25. Angry

26. Arm joint
27. Brother's daughter
28. Small insects
29. Printer's marks
30. Type of wood
31. Girl's name (Fr.)
32. Male cow
34. Sunrises
37. Military rank
38. Mighty
40. Tree fruit
41. Facts

43. Swaps
44. Having a signature
47. Basket, base or foot __
48. Canal or Lake
49. Female spouse
50. Plant base
51. Irish Gaelic
52. Eat
53. Publish
54. Small spots
57. Dove sound

1	2	3	4		5	6	7	8	9		10	11	12	13
14					15						16			
17					18						19			
20				21					22	23				
			24					25						
26	27	28					29					30	31	32
33						34						35		
36				37							38			
39				40					41					
42			43					44						
		45					46							
47	48	49				50	51				52	53	54	
55				56	57					58				
59				60					61					
62				63					64					

PUZZLE 30

ACROSS

1. Male turkeys
5. Lose one's footing
9. Potato (colloq.)
13. Region
14. Make amends
15. Type of grease
16. Tourist site (2 wds.)
19. Spanish cheer
20. Fishing stick
21. Ins and __
22. Transport
23. Set of clothing
25. Not present
28. Curved doorways
31. Embers
32. Animal's disease
34. Pints (abbr.)
36. Filth
37. Sew loosely
38. Warm up
39. Hamilton bill
40. Florida city
41. Question
42. African desert
44. Handbags
45. Receding tides
46. Coin opening
47. Ring of light
49. Thin wood strip

50. Labor union (abbr.)
53. Tourist site (2 wds.)
57. Ammunition (sl.)
58. Flee to wed
59. At a distance
60. Marsh plant
61. Sort; kind
62. __ Horne; singer

DOWN

1. Mexican dish
2. Type of exam
3. Only; bare
4. Girl's nickname
5. Stable section
6. Ore vein
7. Incorporated (abbr.)
8. Pod vegetable
9. Detective
10. Actor's role
11. Vases
12. Dentist's degree (abbr.)
14. Concerning
17. Bridges
18. Speech sound
22. Retained; kept
23. Capital of New Mexico;
    __ Fe
24. Encourage
25. Account (abbr.)

26. Drills
27. Finnish bath
29. Fencing swords
30. Gaze steadily
32. __ and Papas
33. Type of snake
35. Pigpens
37. Fishhook
38. Cause pain
40. Restricted; forbidden
41. Repeat a statement
43. Greetings

44. Aircraft
46. Slant
47. Blood (comb. form)
48. Gifts for the poor
49. Halt
50. Diner
51. Asian country
52. Gumbo vegetable
53. Sweet potato
54. Not dry
55. Crafty
56. Buddy

PUZZLE 31

ACROSS

1. ___ and pepper
5. Ceremony
9. Grinding tooth
14. Smell
15. Send forth
16. Pleasant odor
17. Snout
18. Festive occasion
19. Blackbird
20. Region
21. Years since birth
22. ___ partner
23. Reestablish
25. Tater to Snuffy
26. Unhappy
27. Avoiding extremes
32. Lyricist Gershwin
35. Openly resist authority
37. ___ Empire
38. Plunged into water
40. Gives out
42. Robin or cardinal
43. Signs
45. Baby birds' homes
47. ___ Moines, Iowa
48. Sing for a lover
50. Eighteen wheeler
52. McMahon and Asner
53. Mad scramble (2 wds.)

57. Frightened
61. Five dollar bill (sl.)
62. Nautical below
63. Work
64. Flying aid
65. Ten cents
66. Entertain
67. Otherwise
68. At any time
69. Distributed
70. Buck or doe
71. Complete collections

DOWN

1. Underwater detection
2. Idolize
3. Fails to win
4. Goodies
5. Considered
6. Reflection
7. Baked clay
8. Greek E
9. Seaman
10. Verbal
11. Like extremely
12. Expression of approval
13. Rave
22. Earth
24. Boat paddle
25. Shoe bottoms

27. Group fracas
28. Steal
29. Among
30. Biblical weed
31. Stops
32. Wedding vows (2 wds.)
33. Italian city
34. State positively
36. Buy U.S. Savings __
39. Compass pt. (abbr.)
41. Newcomer
44. Smiled derisively
46. Be seated

49. Increase
51. Report card entries
53. Remove soap
54. Having life
55. Shooting star
56. Water pitchers
57. Close with force
58. Made an appearance
59. Join end to end
60. Fragrant flower
61. Register as a candidate
64. Marry

PUZZLE 32

ACROSS

1. Give off or out
5. Unmixed
9. Take leave (2 wds.)
14. Title
15. Employs
16. Dispute
17. Slightly open
18. Reign
19. Nostrils
20. Gear teeth
21. Crowbar
22. Artist's stands
23. Highest branch
25. Males
26. Railroads (abbr.)
27. Equal in weight
32. Imitate
35. Pine
37. Wait on tables
38. Small boys
40. Draw liquid from
42. Adolescent
43. Speak pompously
45. Wood dye
47. Twisted
48. Souvenirs
50. Halfway
52. Lion's home
53. Accommodates
57. City street
61. Sun
62. Vigor
63. Vitality
64. Light fog
65. Wise
66. Egg shaped
67. Small bills
68. __ Stanley Gardner
69. Walked in water
70. Examination
71. Sly look

DOWN

1. Make into law
2. Military rank
3. Likeness
4. More concise
5. Intended
6. Take by force
7. Depend
8. Wind direction (abbr.)
9. Tropical fruits
10. Periods of time
11. Monster
12. Gas
13. Actor; __ Parker
22. Electric fish
24. Endeavor
25. Obsession

27. Spoiled children
28. Tennis court divider
29. Group of workers
30. Always
31. Disclaim
32. Tiny particle
33. Peel
34. Type of cheese
36. Type of crime
39. Female saint (abbr.)
41. Most agile
44. Lasted
46. Nothing

49. Golf gadget
51. Truck fuel
53. Seeps
54. Stare angrily
55. National bird
56. Show scorn
57. Declare openly
58. Long live (Ital.)
59. Mild oath
60. Short letter
61. Rational
64. Very warm

PUZZLE 33

ACROSS

1. Sluggish
5. Misplaces
10. Bad actor
13. Possess
14. Like very much
15. Wander
16. Dollar bills
17. Of Arctic regions
18. Fermented drinks
19. Dance mate
21. Wave riders
23. Lamprey
24. Send back
25. Frighten
28. Undeveloped flower
29. Auto window sticker
33. Ripped
34. Motor coach
35. Scold severely
36. Farewell
37. Less harsh
39. Tater to Snuffy
40. Leased
42. Ignited
43. Dispatch
44. Look at fixedly
45. Directed
46. Surrenders formally
47. Daisylike flower

49. __ Francisco
50. Motorless planes
53. High seas bandits
57. Vein of ore
58. White bark tree
60. Become weary
61. God of war
62. Stop
63. Garfield's friend
64. __ Moines, Iowa
65. Give financial support
66. Coarse grass

DOWN

1. Visit stores
2. Actress Turner
3. Above
4. Cowboy movie
5. Collar continuation
6. Smell
7. Greek sun god
8. Rubbed out
9. Antitoxin
10. Opening
11. State positively
12. Disarray
15. Roof support
20. Maiden name
22. Passenger
24. Cattle thief

25. Heavenly bodies
26. Want with envy
27. Sandy place
28. Hot dog item
30. Boxed
31. Make amends
32. Grants use of
34. Sleeping room furniture
35. Wager
37. Migratory birds
38. Cover
41. Professions
43. Lawmaker

45. Minimize
46. Automobile
48. Tiny amount
49. Muscular power
50. Pleased
51. Something taught
52. March 15
53. Mexican dollar
54. Help temporarily
55. Great Lake
56. Plant origin
59. Cushion

PUZZLE 34

ACROSS

1. Warbled
5. Petty quarrel
9. Scarlet
12. Tract
13. Attempted
15. Donkey-horse offspring
16. Statutes
17. Addition to contract
18. Being (Lat.)
19. Prankish fairy
20. Young goats
21. Rubbed out
23. __ oil
25. West Indies nation
26. False appearance
27. Incompetent actors (sl.)
28. "People __ Funny"
31. Pools
32. Telegraph code
33. Scold continually
34. Boys
35. Supply with weapons
36. Warship prison
37. Building extension
38. Great happiness
40. Jesters
41. Biblical king of Judah
42. Demolish
43. Extra payment
44. Din
46. Spongelike mushroom
47. Priests or chaplains (sl.)
49. Inventory
50. Finale
53. "MASH" star Alan __
54. Spreads out
56. Greek portico
57. Not excited
58. Subsequently
59. Tiny particle
60. Little barrel
61. Digits of foot
62. Enclosures for animals

DOWN

1. Act of selling
2. __ Sea
3. Large shaggy canine (2 wds.)
4. Fuel
5. Make earnest effort
6. Conceit
7. Helps
8. Golf ball holder
9. Dangerous gamble with revolver (2 wds.)
10. Different
11. Legal document
14. Sleeper's visions
15. Solid food

20. Touch with lips
22. Go up
24. Covers
25. Damages
26. Aims
27. Stallion
29. Train tracks
30. Hens' products
31. Entreaty
32. Yellow
36. Skeletal part
38. Soft white cheese

39. Ropes cattle
40. __ Knox, Ky.
43. Employers
45. Spoken
46. Chop up
47. Deck of cards
48. Medicinal plant
49. Soft meshed fabric
51. Midday
52. Water barriers
55. Hole in ground
56. Juice of tree

PUZZLE 35

ACROSS

1. Smell
5. Curved entry way
9. Short skirt
13. Was a passenger
14. Heavy curtain
15. Dry
16. Patriotic song (3 wds.)
19. 12 month periods (abbr.)
20. On top of
21. Gripper
22. Prayer ending
23. Twirl
25. Crude painter
28. Type of flowers
31. Near the center
32. Stops
34. Imitate
36. Mine entrance
37. Removes from office
38. Again
39. Allow
40. Undercover men
41. Unaccompanied
42. Vender
44. Animal types
45. Hog sound
46. Cuts unevenly
47. Bridge
49. Ballerina skirt
50. Cold virus
53. "I __ allegiance __" (4 wds.)
57. Appraise
58. Binge
59. Cut down a tree
60. Was in debt
61. Pieces out
62. Absent

DOWN

1. Unrestrained indulgence
2. Wall opening
3. __ and ends
4. Confederate soldier; Johnny __
5. Malicious burning
6. File
7. Accountant (abbr.)
8. Skirt edge
9. Service dock
10. Type of flower
11. Pleasant
12. Girl's name
14. Inhibit
17. More crippled
18. Wicked things
22. Aid in crime
23. Narrow cuts
24. Peach centers
25. Use the phone

26. South American mountains
27. Join together
29. Paddle boat
30. Use up
32. Peculiarity
33. Employ
35. Female sheep
37. Unwrap
38. Pub beverages
40. Throw
41. Debate
43. Took on cargo

44. Wash
46. Rope fiber (pl.)
47. Cabbage dish
48. Baseball player; ___ Rose
49. Ripped
50. Soared
51. Tra ___ (hyph.)
52. Unsightly
53. Expert
54. Compass point
55. Route (abbr.)
56. Farm group (abbr.)

PUZZLE 36

ACROSS

1. Period of time
4. Watch pocket
7. Garden tool
10. Animal fat
12. Cloaks
14. Crow calls
15. Understood
16. Group of 8
17. Clue
18. South African fly
20. Fleshy roots
22. Land parcel
23. Senior
24. Blind burrower
26. Chopping tool
27. Halo
30. Toast toppers
31. Spasm
32. Bushwhack
34. Affirmative
35. Calcutta natives
37. 1002
38. Milk product
40. Attempt
41. Pie a la __
42. Status
43. Favorite
44. Uncovered
45. Lukewarm
47. Drunken one
48. Engine-less aircraft
50. Funeral car
53. Healing plant
54. Judge's hammer
56. Belonging to us
58. Graphite
59. Rigid
60. Bird bed
61. Precious stone
62. Consume
63. Witness

DOWN

1. Large deer
2. Talk wildly
3. War god
4. Visage
5. Choose
6. Insect
7. Mane
8. Possesses
9. Time zone (init.)
11. Resides
12. Price
13. Wall support
14. Little angel
19. Foot part
21. Rays
23. Stimulated

24. City official
25. Greek letter
26. Help
28. Gossip
29. Apart
30. Blue bird
31. Explosive (init.)
32. Some
33. Hurry
35. Annoyed
36. Fine skill
39. Loose
41. Married woman

43. Buccaneer
44. Large snake
46. Wooden nails
47. Ego
48. Mirth
49. Rich soil
50. Weight
51. Petitions
52. Irish
53. School subj.
55. Through
57. Saint (Fr.)

PUZZLE 37

ACROSS

1. Bard
5. Frolics
10. At any time
14. Poker stake
15. Labor group
16. Row
17. Sacred image
18. Perceive
19. Opposed (colloq.)
20. Vision aids
22. Stirring device
24. Flower
26. Snow runners
27. Dye
31. Builds
35. Dale ___
36. Cognizant
38. Jackie's 2nd
39. Asks for payment
40. Russian mountains
41. Prompted
42. Fermented drink
43. Not ignited
44. Out of date
45. Places anew
47. Without title
49. Receives after deductions
51. Bun
52. Nice
56. Reverses direction within street
60. Mary's pet
61. Fishing lures
63. ___ Simon; singer
64. Wicked
65. "Peanuts" character
66. ___ Preminger; director
67. Appointment
68. Gladden
69. Hatchery

DOWN

1. Container with handle
2. One time
3. English prep school
4. Anxieties
5. Former U.S.S.R.
6. First number
7. Coin plant
8. Presents a question
9. Tennis shoes
10. Slip by, as time
11. Wine (It.)
12. Inner (comb.)
13. Bridle strap
21. Makes a mistake
23. Father

25. Tangle
27. Closet liner
28. Egg
29. Bowling alleys
30. Mark __; writer
32. Reason
33. Lock of hair
34. Outer edges
37. Place of sacrifice
40. Shaky
41. Ask of one (2 wds.)
43. American Indians

44. Furrier's purchase
46. Make possible
48. Chilled dessert (Fr.)
50. Slug
52. Begged
53. Molten rock
54. Give off
55. __ Turner; singer
57. Merit
58. Cashews
59. Coin depository
62. Egyptian king

1	2	3	4		5	6	7	8	9		10	11	12	13
14					15						16			
17					18						19			
20				21			22			23				
			24			25		26						
27	28	29					30		31			32	33	34
35						36		37				38		
39					40						41			
42				43						44				
45			46				47		48					
			49			50		51						
52	53	54				55		56			57	58	59	
60					61			62			63			
64					65						66			
67					68						69			

PUZZLE 38

ACROSS

1. Thing done
4. __ Moines
7. Father
10. Fake
12. Flames
14. Flooring square
15. Mata __
16. Lawful
17. __ the Terrible
18. Talking bird
20. Man's title
22. Carpet
23. Flower part
24. Press
26. Tuft
27. Sports group
30. Scent
31. Nevertheless
32. Concealed
34. Spider's creation
35. Casual comment
37. Female deer
38. Hammered
40. Adam's mate
41. Salamander
42. Vexed mood (sl.)
43. Weep
44. Automobiles
45. Score

47. Small piece
48. Rhododendron's kin
50. Mechanical men
53. Unlock
54. Baseball teams
56. Pierced ball
58. Extremely
59. Grin
60. Wise
61. Fuss
62. Secret agent
63. Uncooked

DOWN

1. Tree related to olive
2. Fellow
3. Scarlett's home
4. Weight-loss plan
5. Work unit
6. Stitched up
7. Jump into water
8. Having wings
9. Lair
11. Reflector
12. Thrash
13. Narrow opening
14. Named
19. Jog
21. Smooth fabric
23. Earthenware

24. Notions
25. ___ red breast
26. Our star
28. Poisonous snake
29. Cat sounds
30. Possess
31. Sleeping place
32. Garden tool
33. Mesh
35. Copper or tin
36. Climbing vine
39. Earnest prayer
41. Wealthy men

43. Asserts
44. Taxi
46. Camera part
47. Unit of medicine
48. Mimicked
49. Nothing
50. Depend
51. Rip
52. Adventure tale
53. Eggs
55. Sharp bite
57. Morning moisture

PUZZLE 39

ACROSS

1. Sustain
5. Place of shelter
10. Norse god of thunder
14. Roof edge
15. Solitary
16. Wish
17. Irregular 4-sided figure
19. Last
20. Long fish
21. Come to earth
22. Scarcely
23. Village
24. Cozy rooms
25. Total incorrectly
28. Exercise a skill
32. Angry
33. Spacious
34. Neither
35. Periods
36. Water sources
37. Volcanic rock
38. Some
39. Judge's hammer
40. Fork parts
41. Injection devices
43. Swiss or Edam
44. Christmas carol
45. At what time
46. Clefts
49. Animal's den
50. Twosome
53. Indian coin
54. Thinking over
56. Maturing agent
57. A la __
58. Wicked
59. Finest
60. Clothing
61. Festival

DOWN

1. __ Rose, baseball player
2. Unusual
3. Ellipse
4. Energy
5. Danger
6. Onward
7. Null and __
8. Cease
9. Direction (abbr.)
10. Craving for liquid
11. Sharpen
12. Iridescent gem
13. Depend
18. Evade
19. Whim
22. Rays of light
23. Baseball clubs
24. Laughable
25. "Golden Touch" king
26. Sarcasm

27. Woodland deity
28. Long sticks
29. Silly
30. Small bays
31. Rub out
33. Make merry
36. Salary
37. Legal claim
39. Goblin
40. In that place
42. Put in
43. Scolds

45. Desires
46. Crustacean
47. Very large
48. Monkeys
49. Traditional knowledge
50. Jump into water
51. Standard measure
52. Make eyes at
54. Golf goal
55. Boxing official (abbr.)
57. Modern music machine (abbr.)

PUZZLE 40

ACROSS

1. Fine rain
5. On high
10. Madame Bovary
14. Reverberate
15. More recent
16. Post
17. Labor
18. Governess
19. Writer Howard or Ernie
20. Surround
22. Colorful bird
24. Time cycle
25. Gold digger
27. Mechanical man
30. "__ Tin Tin"
31. Banquet
35. A Gershwin
36. Standards
39. London district
40. Old horse
41. Small bite
42. "Ready, __, fire!"
44. Regular (abbr.)
45. Pace
47. Of the sea
49. Beverage
50. Type of fisherman
52. Grassy earth
53. College officials
55. Zany (colloq.)

57. Lubricate
58. Scold
61. Receives willingly
65. And others (abbr.)
66. Cook in liquid
69. Flower container
70. Be appropriate
71. Word with sole or tube
72. Spirit
73. Neat
74. Thick
75. Nowhere person

DOWN

1. Allot
2. Religious painting
3. Knife (sl.)
4. Ohio city
5. Irritate
6. Jump
7. Have
8. Swamp
9. Check for fit (2 wds.)
10. Dominions
11. Sandwich spread, for short
12. Grinding place
13. Sheltered side
21. Caesar's language
23. Game official (abbr.)
25. Type of war casualty (abbr.)
26. Set in, as tile

27. Wash lightly
28. Make a speech
29. Hard roll
30. Meal
32. Large artery
33. Gloss
34. Roman garments
37. Poorly lit
38. Moral wrong
43. Doctor (colloq.)
46. Punishment
48. Rogers or Scheider
51. Groove

54. "Seven come ___"
56. Lukewarm
57. Golden tan
58. Utmost good
59. Needle case
60. Sudden invasion
61. High cards
62. Of slight color
63. Russian ruler (var.)
64. Transmit
67. Singleton
68. Mass. cape

PUZZLE 41

ACROSS

1. Large tailless primates
5. Harvest
9. Less dangerous
14. Long skirt
15. Therefore (Lat.)
16. Pimento stuffed relish
17. Poker stake
18. Rid
19. Stubborn animals
20. Knight's title (pl.)
21. __ Angeles, Calif.
22. Concrete
23. Strew
25. Melancholy
26. Curved line
27. Poker hand
32. Time zone (abbr.)
35. Rome is its capital
37. String toys
38. Gloomy
40. Not fresh
42. __ and away (2 wds.)
43. Movie dog and namesakes
45. Elevated rows
47. Seniors (abbr.)
48. Large hill
50. Employ
52. And so forth (abbr.)
53. __ Tracy, actor

57. Small sofa
61. Pose
62. Story
63. Lag behind
64. Short skirt
65. Ireland (poet.)
66. Male relative
67. Margarine
68. Appraise
69. Inhibit
70. "__ by the Old Mill Stream"
71. Simmer

DOWN

1. Gather
2. Unreasoning fear
3. Spare
4. Midday nap (Sp.)
5. Mirrors
6. Mistake
7. Grows old
8. Edgar Allan __
9. At a future time
10. Astringent ingredient
11. Rasp
12. Tied
13. Relax
22. Automobile
24. Three (pref.)
25. Kind; type

27. Killed
28. Note of indebtedness
29. Cheats (sl.)
30. 60 minute period
31. Teaspoons (abbr.)
32. Kind of cheese
33. Mediocre
34. Ballerina's skirt
36. Garret
39. Raced
41. Volcanic explosion
44. Pittsburgh football player
46. Compass point

49. Dined
51. Goes in
53. Tendon
54. Gem weight
55. Select few
56. Extend a subscription
57. Male breeding animal
58. Sea eagle
59. Diplomacy
60. Ceramic square
61. Grain building
64. Sixties style (abbr.)

PUZZLE 42

ACROSS

1. Revolve extremely fast
5. Strip off
9. Simple liturgical song
14. Knowledge
15. Decorate anew
16. Capital of Vietnam
17. Puts into service
18. Historical periods
19. Rock star John
20. State (suff.)
21. Comedian __ Conway
22. Natural ability
23. High-ranking clergyman
25. Faucet
26. Actor Wallach
27. Advantages
32. Drinking vessel
35. Sour citrus fruit
37. Proportion
38. On upper part
40. Parts in play
42. Adolescent
43. Window glass sections
45. Furry swimming mammal
47. Married woman's title
48. Unethical lawyers (sl.)
50. Swab
52. Yes
53. Of central government
57. Be on guard
61. Vapor
62. Enameled metalware
63. Turn outward
64. Shed
65. Unemployed
66. Eagle's nest
67. Gaelic
68. Yellowish-brown wood
69. Walk on
70. Sly look
71. Very long ages

DOWN

1. Sink suddenly
2. Puzzling problem
3. Performer __ Cara
4. Settle down snuggly
5. More delicately attractive
6. Spooky
7. Mild yellow cheese
8. __ Angeles, Calif.
9. Less expensive
10. Corridor
11. Poker stake
12. 12 o'clock daytime
13. Color slightly
22. Light brown
24. Entire number
25. Principle

27. Lightning flashes
28. Greasy
29. Article
30. Layer
31. Male children to parent
32. Beanies and others
33. Mountain State
34. Small horse
36. Mary Tyler __
39. Foot (Zool.)
41. Half school year
44. Began
46. Straight stick

49. Organ of sight
51. Trim and small
53. Untrue
54. Cowboys' exhibition
55. Edgar __ Poe
56. Onionlike vegetables
57. Pound
58. Always
59. Form of be
60. Operatic melody
61. Tapering cloth piece
64. Singer Torme

PUZZLE 43

ACROSS

1. Father
5. Near
10. Firewood
13. Frosted
14. West Indies nation
15. Go on horseback
16. Mine railway car
17. Loafed
18. Common metal
19. Novels published in parts
21. Well-being
23. Relieve (of)
24. Wild
25. Lance
28. Container for peas
29. Poke fun at
33. High
34. Attila the __
35. Bed canopy
36. Consumed food
37. Boxer's trainer
39. Soft metal
40. Wealth
42. Meadow (poet.)
43. Dimensions
44. Entire amount
45. Wager
46. Confronts squarely
47. Beg

49. Modern
50. Hold up
53. Ice cream confections
57. Small island
58. Furry swimming animal
60. Reverse doing
61. College head
62. Shuts with force
63. Footfall
64. A standard time (abbr.)
65. Spooky
66. $10 bills (colloq.)

DOWN

1. Holes or shafts in ground
2. Land measure
3. Soft juicy fruit
4. High-ranking naval officer
5. Human offspring
6. Boys
7. Petroleum
8. Cooked slowly
9. Large sea duck
10. Money of Italy
11. Smell
12. Hereditary factor
15. Shoulder guns
20. Breeze
22. After some time
24. Caressed

25. Begin
26. Paved house area
27. Choose by vote
28. Play on words
30. Garret
31. Grab
32. Sea eagles
34. Possesses
35. Orange pekoe
37. Word of greeting
38. Allow
41. Occur
43. Tiny particles of wood

45. Fight in a war
46. Bog
48. Irregular
49. Surgeon's assistant
50. Flank
51. Employs
52. Map of lots
53. Partly (pref.)
54. Poker stake
55. Paradise
56. Soaks in liquid
59. Dark sticky substance

PUZZLE 44

ACROSS

1. Of the ear
5. Duck's graceful relatives
10. Healthy
14. Cry of 1-down
15. Color the walls
16. Surrounded by
17. Grassy yard
18. Command
19. Intertwined
20. Depots
22. Rouse from sleep
24. Hotel
25. Roman numeral 8
26. Smells bad
29. Animal that eats
    its own kind
33. Less
34. Governed
35. Trouble
36. Inactive
37. Small drum
38. Farm yield
39. Peggy or pinky
40. Cut off
41. Flee to wed
42. Regarded highly
44. Odors
45. Licks up

46. __ la la
47. Hurtful remark
50. Teemed
55. Sow
56. Eskimo's house
58. Tender
59. Solitary
60. Of the nose
61. __ Fitzgerald; singer
62. Finishes
63. Total income
64. Antlered animal

DOWN

1. Nocturnal birds of prey
2. This and __
3. Hawkeye State
4. Resume
5. Knives, forks and __
6. Caution
7. Helps
8. Compass point
9. Filter
10. Honolulu's state
11. In a frenzied state
12. "One life to __"
13. Paradise
21. Writing fluids
23. Breeze

25. Heroism
26. Grin
27. Ebb and flow
28. Bay
29. Diced
30. British noble
31. Take as one's own
32. Canter like-gaits
34. Rants
37. Enticing
38. Washed
40. Close securely

41. Light tan
43. Escapes detection
44. Backless eats
47. Small island
48. Gas light
49. Remit
50. Too
51. Large snakes
52. Give sparingly
53. ___ Stanley Gardner
54. Precious
57. Needlefish

1	2	3	4		5	6	7	8	9		10	11	12	13
14					15						16			
17					18						19			
20				21					22	23				
			24				25							
26	27	28				29					30	31	32	
33					34					35				
36				37					38					
39				40				41						
42			43				44							
			45				46							
47	48	49				50	51				52	53	54	
55				56	57				58					
59				60					61					
62				63					64					

PUZZLE 45

ACROSS

1. Young cow
5. Speed contest
9. Indian tent
14. Aroma
15. Ardor
16. Piano key
17. Crazy (sl.)
18. Climbing plant
19. Nervous
20. Type of exam
21. Eisenhower's nickname
22. Smoothed lumber
23. East
25. Small kettle
26. Accountant (abbr.)
27. Threatening
32. Skill
35. By oneself
37. Task
38. Become a member
40. Watermelon piece
42. Lake or Canal
43. Assign
45. Perfect
47. Terminate
48. Get back
50. Make free
52. Robert E. or Pinky
53. Worked dough

57. A short time
61. Hawaiian food
62. Close by
63. Red, __ and blue
64. Set fire to
65. Animal pen
66. Type of duck
67. Boast
68. __ Fitzgerald
69. Woman's garment
70. Franklin and Casey
71. Flower stalk

DOWN

1. Liveliness
2. Worship
3. Topical
4. Romp
5. Religious meetings
6. The same as
7. Sugar stalk
8. Wind direction (abbr.)
9. Having great size and power
10. Level
11. Small lake
12. Irish Gaelic
13. Ogled
22. __ Fernando Valley
24. Ecology group (abbr.)
25. Part

27. Insinuating
28. That girl
29. Ripped
30. Ireland
31. Type of grass
32. Slightly open
33. Actor's part
34. Slope
36. Martini garnish
39. Neither this __ that
41. Wages
44. Cultivators
46. Falsehood

49. Wide shoe size
51. Waltz and Tango
53. Moslem's sacred book
54. Distributed
55. American bird
56. Sleep image
57. Filled with respect
58. Buzzing sound
59. Conceal
60. Residents (suff.)
61. Unmixed
64. Business group (abbr.)

PUZZLE 46

ACROSS

1. Something circular
5. Ordinary language
10. Dry plant fuel
14. Region
15. Rental contract
16. Tra ___ (2 wds.)
17. Lion's yell
18. Come in
19. Epochal
20. Beg
22. Type of print
24. Consume
25. Smiles evilly
27. Obligations
30. Ocean
31. Bread ingredient
35. Exist
36. Complete
39. Small coin
40. Paving substance
41. Lion constellation
42. 40 winks
44. Loud noise
45. Utilizes
47. Commands
49. Summer (Fr.)
50. Measure of length
52. Amongst
53. Thing of value
55. Poem part
57. Work at steadily
58. Arm covering
61. Animals with hair
65. Tresses
66. Flower part
69. Political coalition
70. Gumbo vegetable
71. Elude
72. ___ Preminger
73. Pare
74. Subsequently
75. Misplaced

DOWN

1. Unusually fine
2. Press
3. Orderly
4. Attic
5. Pressed fold
6. Lease
7. Cereal grain
8. Direction (abbr.)
9. Weird
10. Gratified
11. British nobleman
12. Jai ___; handball
13. Powder
21. Artist's stand
23. Attempt
25. Hawaiian garland
26. Worked for

27. Piece of information

28. Rub out

29. French cap

30. Tempests

32. Military assistants

33. Strike

34. Principle

37. New (pref.)

38. Hearing organ

43. Sacred song

46. Quite a few

48. Pass away

51. Pastor (abbr.)

54. Emblem

56. Drive away

57. Whiter

58. Store

59. Tahoe or Erie

60. Ireland

61. Created

62. Low female voice

63. Plenty

64. Edinburgh native

67. __ Gabor

68. Make lace

PUZZLE 47

ACROSS

1. In a different way
5. Manage
9. Serving piece
13. Essence
14. Sweetener
15. Ritual
16. TV family? (2 wds.)
19. Cloth measures (abbr.)
20. Medicine measure
21. __ facto
22. Roofing piece
23. Hair style
25. Gun cleaner
28. Sewing necessity
31. Narcotic
32. Mooed
34. Consume
36. Colt's mother
37. __ wave
38. The Wise Men
39. Fine craft
40. Bread man
41. Woven cotton
42. Three times
44. Trade
45. Raw steel
46. Cast a ballot
47. Jargon
49. Cattle (Arch.)
50. Cereal grain
53. Traveler's purchase (2 wds.)
57. Impolite
58. Margarines
59. Penny
60. Time cycle
61. Look narrowly
62. Oak or elm

DOWN

1. Catch sight of
2. Noisy
3. Stand-ins, for short
4. Building wing
5. Imprecation
6. Curved molding
7. Buddy
8. Age
9. Camera stand
10. Rivers (Sp.)
11. __ time; never (2 wds.)
12. Affirmative
14. Upbraid
17. Dialect
18. Wearied
22. Factual
23. __ Sadat
24. Sense

25. European capital (It.)
26. Separated
27. Laughter
29. Smallest
30. Bird of prey
32. Compare
33. Poem of praise
35. Layer
37. Mexican snack
38. Mud
40. Beginning
41. Anon
43. Look-alike (sl.)

44. Extra reward
46. Cap feature
47. Hint
48. Verdi opera
49. Leg joint
50. Unique thing
51. Skin problem
52. Head (Fr.)
53. Cook in oil
54. Peak
55. Island (Fr.)
56. Play segment

PUZZLE 48

ACROSS

1. Fitted with shoes
5. Applauds
10. Rubbish heap
14. Small inlet
15. Greeting
16. Jacob's twin (Bib.)
17. Chimp and orang
18. Lazy person
19. Exam
20. Of the mind
22. Takes into custody
24. Goes on horseback
27. Aye
28. One tending horses
31. __ Vegas, Nev.
33. Thong
37. Sacred
38. Food fish
40. The self
41. Strange
42. Father (colloq.)
43. Greek goddess of dawn
44. Needlefish
45. Visualize
46. Not straight
48. __ recorder
49. Rich cake
51. Drink in bits
52. Receipts in business

53. Devoured
55. Valuable thing
57. Work of highest excellence
61. Fasten to
65. Takes unlawfully
66. Giver
69. Writer __ Stanley Gardner
70. Fencing sword
71. Oxlike antelope
72. Back part
73. Water source
74. Shoes violent anger
75. Sensible

DOWN

1. Confidence game (sl.)
2. Expect and want
3. Baking chamber
4. Demolish
5. Baby
6. Conducted
7. Every one
8. Entreaty
9. Regretful
10. Hate
11. Employs
12. "Two Years Before the __"
13. Places
21. Goal
23. Stops working
25. Escapes notice

26. "My Gal __"
28. Shadowy apparition
29. Cowboy's exhibition
30. More mature
32. Slumbers
34. Of kings
35. Wide open
36. Tiny skin openings
38. Human race
39. Very long age
42. Musical works for two
47. By way of
48. Ragged clothes

50. Hanging thread ornament
52. Television receiver
54. Large sea duck
56. Orange-red stones
57. Group working together
58. Swinging stride
59. Cain's brother (Bib.)
60. Carbonated soft drink
62. Region
63. Related Scottish group
64. In this place
67. Find fault constantly
68. Single

PUZZLE 49

ACROSS

1. Woe is me!
5. Treatment
10. Records (abbr.)
13. Impression
14. Bare figures
15. Drill hole
16. Appointment
17. Presses
18. Earth science (abbr.)
19. "Jeffersons" or "Rhoda"
21. Quickly pen a letter (2 wds.)
23. Shed tears
24. Holds the __ puzzle (2 wds.)
25. Attractive girl (sl.)
28. Knight's title
29. Main artery
33. Cain's brother
34. Towel embroidery
35. Bids
36. Reagan to Nancy
37. Lops (2 wds.)
39. After Fri.
40. Sampled food
42. Type of grain
43. Walk in water
44. Rob
45. Not on duty
46. Bring down
47. "Digger" Barnes' son
49. Set
50. Start of football game
53. Shirker (sl., hyph.)
57. Wicked
58. Safe cracker's explosive
60. Small island
61. Nathan nickname
62. "Deep six" location
63. Foot cover
64. Single unit
65. Swarms
66. Witches

DOWN

1. Finds a sum
2. Vault
3. Against
4. Lettering cutout
5. Bring together
6. Sea surge
7. Fuss
8. Sex
9. School paper
10. Crazy (sl.)
11. College teacher (colloq.)
12. Ego
15. Behalf (obs.)
20. Mined product
22. Group of assistants
24. Abrupt dismissal (sl.)

25. Golf vehicles
26. Submarine
27. On edge
28. Pose for portrait
30. Recut board
31. Swap
32. Fall flower
34. Newman movie
35. Often (poet.)
37. Stringed instrument
38. Lout
41. Bring down at knees
43. Predatory

45. Indoor work place
46. Constellation
48. Unless (2 wds.)
49. Thugs (sl.)
50. Vegas game
51. __ the Terrible
52. Refer to
53. Metric weight unit
54. Government safety agcy.
55. Beat with whip
56. Professional charges
59. Golf peg

PUZZLE 50

ACROSS

1. Burn to charcoal
5. Telephone
9. The devil
14. Entice
15. Raw metals
16. Nimble
17. Leave out
18. Loan
19. Indian tent
20. Space agency (abbr.)
21. __ Vegas
22. Failed to hit
23. Foes
25. Female sibling
26. And so on (abbr.)
27. Radioactive measure
32. Possesses
35. Sipping device
37. Arabian country
38. __ Fitzgerald
40. Glutted
42. Mimicked
43. Posts
45. Closed car
47. Avenues (abbr.)
48. Racer's rests (2 wds.)
50. Pad
52. Overhead trains
53. Shows up

57. Swapped
61. Fruit beverage
62. On the ocean
63. Turbine
64. Black
65. Window part
66. Make amends
67. Simple
68. Prepare copy
69. Sulked
70. Sleigh
71. Groups

DOWN

1. Appears to be a copy
2. Member of mankind
3. Get up
4. Domesticate again
5. Gathers
6. Regions
7. Camera part
8. Psychedelic drug (abbr.)
9. Gratify fully
10. Grows older
11. Gratuities
12. Toward shelter
13. Require
22. Wire measure
24. That thing's
25. Cut wood

27. Detests
28. Meadow
29. Little devils
30. Length measures
31. Ceases
32. Rope fiber
33. Jai __; handball
34. Narrow opening
36. Files
39. Capone, et al.
41. Moistened
44. Guided
46. 40 winks

49. Ancient
51. Pesters
53. Love
54. Stage whisper
55. Set afire again
56. Seasons
57. Streetcar
58. Turning (pref.)
59. On
60. Finished
61. Cain's brother
64. Print measures

1	2	3	4	■	5	6	7	8	■	9	10	11	12	13
14				■	15				■	16				
17				■	18				■	19				
20				■	21			■	22					
23			24			■	25			■	■	■	■	■
■	■	26			■	27			28	29	30	31
32	33	34	■	35		36		■	37			
38			39	■	40			41	■	42		
43				44	■	45			46	■	47	
48				49		■	50		51	■	■	■
■	■	■	52			■	53			54	55	56
57	58	59	60			■	61			■	62	
63				■	64			■	65			
66				■	67			■	68			
69				■	70			■	71			

PUZZLE 51

ACROSS

1. Line
4. Food fish
7. Mineral spring
10. Enthusiastic
12. Got along
14. Loved one
15. Nothing more than
16. Sandy place
17. Sunrise direction
18. Speak from memory
20. Not us
22. High card
23. Vapor
24. Bounding line
26. Reverential fear
27. Two make a score
30. Eminence
31. Before now
32. Make smaller
34. Actress Gardner
35. Read letter by letter
37. __ Jones Industrials
38. Entertain lavishly
40. Boy
41. Fairy tale monster
42. Remove from print
43. Not many
44. Forest member
45. Automobile turned sour

47. Crumpled paper
48. Plundered
50. Take into custody
53. Chair
54. An old saying
56. 500 sheets of paper
58. Hearing organs
59. Fits into a mortise
60. Lower price offer
61. Paid notices
62. Eighteen wheeler
63. Permit

DOWN

1. Male sheep
2. Above
3. Cable
4. Feel concern
5. Metal source
6. Indicate
7. Scorch
8. Go by
9. Creative work
11. Ten year period
12. Destiny
13. Calendar reading
14. Decreed
19. Skating surface
21. Disliked
23. Enlarged

24. Put money away
25. Reflection
26. Years since birth
28. Push gently
29. Twenty
30. Distant
31. Gorilla
32. Bright color
33. Female sheep
35. Freezing rain
36. Enforceable rule
39. Gives shares
41. Commands

43. Cornstalks
44. Sticky substance
46. Beef or pork
47. Small bird
48. Direct the course
49. Boat paddles
50. Excited
51. Close with molten wax
52. Story
53. Large body of water
55. Black bird
57. Encountered

PUZZLE 52

ACROSS

1. Actor Holbrook
4. Armed conflict
7. Tangle together
10. Military subdivision
12. Capital of France
14. Money paid employee
15. Rip
16. Tie or scarf
17. Mental image
18. Sudden sharp twist
20. Detects flavor
22. Actress __ West
23. Roost
24. Large circular band
26. Cushion
27. Lampreys and morays
30. Soft juicy fruit
31. Hawaiian flower garland
32. Increase wealth of
34. Mooselike deer
35. Sincere
37. Mountain (comb.)
38. Finds out gradually
40. Make lace
41. Bite suddenly
42. Burden
43. Wager
44. Inhale suddenly
45. Underground plant stem
47. Massage
48. Stick together
50. Givers
53. __ sapiens
54. Map book
56. Actress __ Louise
58. Always
59. Stare fiercely
60. Pack away
61. Fellows
62. Watch
63. Female sheep

DOWN

1. Small temporary dwelling
2. Again
3. Fibber
4. Cleanse with water
5. Circle part
6. Took part in uproar
7. Constructed
8. Matures
9. Steeped beverage
11. A shaking
12. Walk to and fro
13. Heavenly body
14. Shrivel
19. Sleep briefly
21. Fragrance
23. Rembrandt, for one

24. Word of greeting
25. Made of hardwood
26. For each
28. Big cats
29. Old metal
30. Round __ in square hole
31. __ Vegas, Nev.
32. A standard time (abbr.)
33. Short leap
35. Come afterward
36. Devour
39. Writer
41. Wooden shoes

43. Kind of bug
44. Pistol
46. Boast
47. __ of Sharon
48. Small bay
49. Sign of future
50. Challenge
51. Ceremony
52. Cold white flakes
53. Garment border
55. Put down
57. Fearful respect

PUZZLE 53

ACROSS

1. Valuable stone
4. Wager
7. Policeman (sl.)
10. Draft animals
12. Whiskers
14. Change residence
15. Terrible
16. Go in
17. Prayer ending
18. Gave examinations
20. Expert
22. Crag
23. Mechanical being
24. Assist
26. For each
27. For fear that
30. Bottom of foot
31. Sack
32. Separated
34. __ Baba
35. Seaman
37. Military address (abbr.)
38. Caressed
40. Earthenware cup
41. Proper
42. Close tightly
43. Rooster's mate
44. Unwanted plant
45. Wise lawmaker
47. Dog's foot
48. Kitty's favorite mint
50. Middle
53. "Arsenic and Old __"
54. Treat with mercy
56. Mild yellow cheese
58. Dry and barren
59. Pavarotti's voice
60. Ceremony
61. Marry
62. Tear
63. Decade

DOWN

1. Supreme being
2. Way out
3. Only
4. Curve
5. Consume food
6. A shaking
7. Approach
8. Above
9. Corral
11. Cuddle
12. Alcoholic drink
13. Dull
14. As a __ of fact
19. Upper part
21. Of the sun
23. Regulated health system
24. Pits
25. Select group

26. Average
28. Look fixedly
29. Lukewarm
30. Weaken
31. Unfavorable
32. Projecting pin
33. Comedian __ DeLuise
35. Cantaloupe
36. Convent sister
39. Tried for flavor
41. Silvery-gray alloy
43. Funnel-shaped container

44. Pale
46. Inventory
47. Equal
48. Feel concern
49. Sour
50. Agricultural product
51. Prepare for publication
52. Charge per unit
53. Statue
55. Black cuckoo
57. Fellows

PUZZLE 54

ACROSS

1. Mata __
5. British peninsula
10. Charts
14. Black
15. Angry
16. Medicinal herb
17. Cried
18. Object
19. Chromosome part
20. Arm covering
22. Went forward
24. File
26. Ireland
27. Woodsman
31. Leash
35. Get up
36. Grain towers
38. Singular
39. Fluff
40. Engine
41. Attractive (sl.)
42. Tree trunk section
43. Founded
44. Facilitated
45. Slept loudly
47. Colonists
49. British college
51. Rational
52. Desecrates
56. Fortuitous
60. Crippled
61. Saltpeter
63. Food shop
64. Declare
65. Quartz stone
66. Prayer ending
67. Strong desires
68. Fragment
69. American Beauty

DOWN

1. Shapes with an axe
2. Cain's brother
3. Thick cord
4. Curiosity
5. Broadest
6. Exist
7. Buddhist priest
8. Musical study
9. Attendant
10. Lodestone
11. __ Guinness
12. Corn bread
13. Source
21. Flower holder
23. Greek god of war
25. Spanish coins

27. Drops
28. Hunter constellation
29. Beatle __ Starr
30. Ceremonials
32. Dwelling place
33. Come in
34. Hollow grasses
37. Metallic veins
40. Virgin Mary statues
41. Date chart
43. Type of VCR
44. Sicilian volcano

46. Alludes
48. __ and feathered
50. Horse sound
52. Frolic
53. Rant
54. Portent
55. Celebrity
57. Exhibit item (sl.)
58. Bull ring cheers
59. Ore source
62. Summer (Fr.)

PUZZLE 55

ACROSS

1. Commit robbery
4. Plant juice
7. Actor Holbrook
10. Offensive to look at
12. Receipts in business
14. Peace symbol
15. Sky color
16. Twine about
17. Secondhand
18. Rubs out
20. Interfere with
22. Male sheep
23. Untamed
24. __ ads
26. Evergreen
27. Microorganism
30. "Star __"
31. Human being
32. Fairies
34. Help
35. Devilish
37. Large tank
38. Actress De Carlo
40. Loiter
41. Numerous
42. Pa. port city
43. Crafty
44. Buddies
45. Unpleasant
47. Distant
48. Submissively
50. Distort (a story)
53. 1/2 quart
54. With normal voice
56. Den
58. Actor __ Griffith
59. Concise
60. Light tan
61. Aye
62. Fix in position
63. Range of knowledge

DOWN

1. Polish
2. Make eyes at
3. Smear
4. Cuts lumber
5. __ Baba
6. Vex
7. Stockings
8. Assert
9. Conducted
11. Longs for
12. Stalk
13. Featured performer
14. Two-family house
19. Rested on chair
21. Mysterious power
23. In conclusion

24. Give up (a right)
25. Passion
26. Grease
28. Competitor
29. Agency
30. Route
31. __ West; life preserver vest
32. Hog
33. Pen for 32-down
35. Move stealthily
36. Negative vote
39. XC
41. Hard limestone

43. Fashions
44. Equal status
46. Venetian blind strip
47. Lose color
48. Belonging to me
49. Finishes
50. Strong rush of air
51. Deficiency
52. Ireland's former name
53. Settle debt
55. Combination of minerals
57. Gallop

PUZZLE 56

ACROSS

1. Join to something else
4. Earth (pref.)
7. Fodder
10. Orderly
12. Funeral chant
14. Strong wind
15. Appointment
16. Russian mountains
17. Raw metals
18. __ in the Lion's Den
20. Slanted type
22. Negative
23. Trap
24. Foreleg
26. Thick mist
27. Both (pref.)
30. Monkeys
31. Buddy
32. Preoccupy
34. Deceased on arrival (abbr.)
35. Dots
37. Double curve
38. Soaked
40. Father
41. Genuine
42. Greek instrument
43. Large deer kin
44. Medicine unit
45. Tusk material

47. English beverage
48. Donors
50. Throat part
53. Underground chamber
54. Bird claw
56. __ the line; behaved
58. Tent maker
59. Mixes up
60. Celebrity
61. London's Big __
62. Buddhist sect
63. Some

DOWN

1. Conjunction
2. Inanimate
3. Information
4. Lass
5. Epoch
6. Making eyes at
7. Mata __
8. __ Guinness
9. Affirmative
11. Racket game
12. Song for two
13. This (Sp.)
14. Fake humans
19. Charged particle
21. Desert dwellers
23. Compactly

24. Thread holder
25. Intoxicating
26. At a distance
28. Tavern beverages
29. Edition
30. Commercials
31. Writing instrument
32. Strange
33. Direction (abbr.)
35. Annoy
36. Hardwood tree
39. Auto controller
41. Browns bread

43. Makeshift
44. Lair
46. Food bits
47. Heavy weights
48. Amusing contest
49. __ the Terrible
50. Ripped
51. Jot
52. Thin
53. Corn holder
55. Prevaricate
57. Arid

PUZZLE 57

ACROSS

1. Smash
5. Triangular skirt inserts
10. Sailing vessel
14. On protected side (naut.)
15. Representative
16. Large food fish
17. __ cat
18. Open space in woods
19. Against (pref.)
20. Expose to harm
22. Magazine department head
24. "For Me and My __"
25. Box in exhibition
26. Recessed section of room
29. Fence of stakes
33. Unsophisticated (colloq.)
34. Valleys
35. Performer __ Vereen
36. Digits of foot
37. Ventures
38. Baptismal basin
39. Wind direction (abbr.)
40. Sturdy fabric
41. Sot
42. Uses up gradually
44. President Jimmy __
45. Dollar bills
46. Mineral

47. Makes hoglike sounds
50. Short distance runner
55. Thick strong cord
56. Bird's claw
58. Father
59. Image of god
60. Call forth
61. Flower
62. Declare untrue
63. Discourage from doing
64. Penny

DOWN

1. Knighted title, female
2. Actor Alda
3. Transmit
4. Six-sided figures
5. Flock of geese
6. Make eyes at
7. Back part
8. Conclusion
9. Spires
10. Steps
11. Pursue game
12. Division word
13. Two
21. Nation's sea force
23. Raised platform
25. Oregon's capital

26. Played a role
27. Not tight
28. Crawl along ground
29. Capital of France
30. All around
31. Compact
32. Come into
34. Copenhagen natives
37. Hated
38. Of public debate
40. Slight hollow
41. Hindu woman's garment

43. Solitary
44. Where streets meet
47. Network of bars
48. Went in vehicle
49. Once __ a time...
50. Slit for coin
51. Jab
52. Grow weary
53. Ireland (poet.)
54. Sleep
57. Hail!

1	2	3	4		5	6	7	8	9		10	11	12	13
14					15						16			
17					18						19			
20				21					22	23				
			24					25						
26	27	28					29					30	31	32
33						34					35			
36					37					38				
39				40					41					
42			43					44						
			45					46						
47	48	49					50	51			52	53	54	
55					56	57				58				
59					60					61				
62					63					64				

PUZZLE 58

ACROSS

1. Bounding gait
5. Open space in forest
10. Singer-actor Burl __
14. Iridescent stone
15. Red-breasted thrush
16. River through Egypt
17. Peddle
18. Expert
19. Waistcoat
20. Agreement between nations
22. Rubs out
24. Fish eggs
25. Sunk in mud
27. Highest point
30. ___ Franklin
31. Jeans fabric
35. Actor __ Harrison
36. Develop gradually
39. __ ranch; vacation resort
40. Street (abbr.)
41. Break moral law
42. __ Jima; Pacific island
44. Small cozy room
45. Ermine and mink
47. Dissolved
49. Wander idly
50. Grand __ National Park, Wyo.
52. Kind of bread
53. Clothe
55. Rental contract
57. Arafat's organization (abbr.)
58. Leaves of grass
61. Stabbing weapon on rifle
65. Rajah's wife
66. Glossy fabric
69. Auction
70. Poker stake
71. Raise spirits of
72. Flooring piece
73. Rip
74. Prongs
75. Shut with force

DOWN

1. Warm attachment
2. Unfold
3. Breathe heavily
4. Older persons
5. Scrape into particles
6. Rich ore vein
7. Short for Abraham
8. Immerse
9. Go into
10. Pushed in hostilely
11. Competes
12. Other
13. Mounts gem
21. Memos
23. Crimson
25. Singer __ Tillis
26. Ask to come

27. Special skill
28. Musical show
29. Apply oneself
30. Silly blunders (sl.)
32. Gentle push
33. Thoughts
34. Repairs
37. Vigor
38. Female sheep
43. Strangely
46. Army member
48. Strong alkaline substance
51. Before marriage

54. Perches for birds
56. Valuable thing
57. Window glass sections
58. Unruly child
59. Narrow way
60. Square column
61. Pierce with teeth
62. Spike
63. Singer Fitzgerald
64. Swarm
67. __ Baba
68. Convert to leather

PUZZLE 59

ACROSS

1. Strike noisily
5. Range
10. "My Gal __"
13. Was a passenger
14. Slender candle
15. Evergreen tree
16. Declare
17. Subsequently to
18. Within
19. Communication
21. Sea trips
23. Frost
24. Summer TV fare
25. Sired
28. Pea container
29. Slack
33. Portent
34. Ocean
35. Bother
36. Was victorious
37. Reflectors
39. Soft metal
40. Musical studies
42. Wedding response (2 wds.)
43. Chromosome part
44. Bowling alley button
45. Conjunction
46. Grows weary
47. Existence
49. Paving substance
50. Comes back
53. Fell heavily
57. __ the Terrible
58. Cognizant
60. Molten rock
61. Not well
62. At no time
63. Paradise
64. Large deer kin
65. Rub out
66. Rational

DOWN

1. Eat greedily
2. Adore
3. Fruit beverages
4. Iranian
5. Actor's platform
6. Restaurant
7. Choose
8. Annoyed
9. Mistake
10. Vocalize
11. Poker stake
12. Lion signs
15. Keyboard instruments
20. Behave
22. Christmases
24. Bellowing

25. Arbor
26. Show feeling
27. Class
28. For each
30. Aquatic animal
31. Fishing net
32. Sea birds
34. Female sibling
35. __ and con
37. Length measure
38. Strange
41. Show errors
43. Corsets

45. Response
46. Greek T
48. Foolish
49. In that place
50. Go up
51. Wicked
52. Small nail
53. Three (Sp.)
54. Infant's 1st word
55. Smooth
56. Denmark native
59. Hummingbird

1	2	3	4		5	6	7	8	9		10	11	12
13					14						15		
16					17						18		
19				20				21		22			
			23				24						
25	26	27				28				29		30	31	32
33					34				35				
36				37				38				39	
40			41				42				43		
44						45				46			
			47		48				49				
50	51	52					53				54	55	56
57					58		59				60		
61					62						63		
64					65						66		

UZZLE 60

ACROSS

1. Record players
4. Opening
7. Eureka
10. Deceased
12. Lubricated
14. Shank
15. Far (pref.)
16. Curtain
17. Evergreen tree
18. Writing instrument
20. Dot
22. Male offspring
23. Lukewarm
24. Get rid of
26. Make a mistake
27. Relate
30. Burn
31. Hummingbird
32. Antenna
34. Piece of butter
35. Medicine men
37. Raw metal
38. Experts
40. Place
41. Writing fluids
42. Jacob's brother
43. Kind
44. Throw
45. Silly

47. 1st workday (abbr.)
48. Camera parts
50. Of the sea
53. Transmitted
54. Is a passenger
56. Enthusiasm
58. Cushions
59. Scents
60. Not difficult
61. Commercials
62. Female sheep
63. Rural address abbreviations

DOWN

1. Long-lasting insecticide
2. Army vehicle
3. Bargain event
4. Lass
5. According to (2 wds.)
6. Hot seasoning
7. Buckeye State
8. Female deer
9. Singular
11. More compact
12. Chief Norse god
13. Profound
14. Black Widow
19. Food fish
21. Ceremonials
23. Walk on

24. Tint
25. Detests
26. ___ Gabor
28. Jungle kings
29. Songbirds
30. Accountant (abbr.)
31. Satisfied sounds
32. Picnic pest
33. French article
35. Dazes
36. Arctic bird
39. Applies color
41. Charge electrically

43. Within
44. Peak
46. Air (pref.)
47. Catholic service
48. Guide
49. Ceases
50. Simple
51. Close
52. Sunrise direction
53. Health resort
55. Economy measure
57. Soap ingredient

PUZZLE 61

ACROSS

1. Hoarseness
5. Letter requirement
10. Tranquil
14. Roof edge
15. Teach
16. Towards shelter
17. Actor Alda
18. Battery terminal (neg.)
19. Lion's sound
20. Message by wire
22. Dairy product
24. Big mouse
25. Dregs
26. Leftovers
29. Avoid
33. Select group
34. Dug from earth
35. Tavern drink
36. Wander
37. Broadcasted
38. Jogging gait
39. Employ
40. Not as young
41. Grasp for
42. Highest point
44. Man's hat
45. Two female deer
46. Black bird

47. Large cave
50. Physical power
55. Operatic solo
56. Watch for
58. Great Lake
59. Stagger about
60. Mark over a vowel
61. Small stream
62. Go by
63. Go in
64. Foot movement

DOWN

1. Notable deed
2. Harsh breathing sound
3. __ Office
4. Bring into being
5. Begins
6. Food fish
7. Particle
8. Youthful fad
9. Went before
10. Stroke lovingly
11. African lily
12. Meadows
13. Nothing more than
21. Stare with mouth open
23. Listen to
25. Passenger ship

26. Antitoxin
27. Cease doing business
28. Large steam
29. Warning device
30. Fortune telling card
31. Flee to marry
32. Name for a rabbit
34. King with a golden touch
37. Cause to be unfriendly
38. Animal instructors
40. Smell
41. Moved away

43. Goals
44. Trade
47. Freshwater fish
48. Region
49. Competes
50. Seasoning
51. Help temporarily
52. Bravery
53. Baked clay
54. Assist
57. Emerge victorious

1	2	3	4		5	6	7	8	9		10	11	12	13
14					15						16			
17					18						19			
20				21					22	23				
			24					25						
26	27	28					29					30	31	32
33						34					35			
36					37						38			
39				40					41					
42			43					44						
		45						46						
47	48	49				50	51				52	53	54
55				56	57				58				
59				60					61				
62				63					64				

PUZZLE 62

ACROSS

1. Formal school dance
5. Snapshot
10. Automobiles
14. Talk wildly
15. Actor __ Moore
16. One
17. Frosted
18. Young owl
19. Actress Hayworth
20. Can be repaired
22. Shout (colloq.)
24. Untruth
25. Indefinite amount
26. Tears into pieces
29. Path for pedestrians
33. Equals
34. Parlor
35. Gain victory
36. Priests' white robes
37. A flower
38. Glut
39. Four-in-hand
40. Venetian blind strips
41. Thick smooth soup
42. Being alone
44. Frisks
45. Eat
46. High mountain

47. Return to old ways
50. Marks against student
55. Orient
56. Leave out
58. Prepare for publication
59. Enclosed shopping center
60. Fray
61. Tender
62. Brings suit in court
63. Stretches across
64. A lot (colloq.)

DOWN

1. Stiffly formal
2. Speed contest
3. Baking chamber
4. Those who interfere
5. Investigates
6. Wolf's wailing cry
7. Make eyes at
8. Golf ball holder
9. Conventional
10. Brownish wading bird
11. Plant source of indigo
12. Ceremony
13. Featured performer
21. Assists
23. Portent
25. Farm towers

26. Coverings for instep & ankle
27. Sun (comb.)
28. Revolt
29. Saline
30. Realizing
31. Metric unit, 1.06 liquid qt.
32. Joints of legs
34. Use with others
37. Farmers
38. Put down by force
40. Mix with spoon
41. Wan

43. Noble goals
44. Humped animals
47. Drives into
48. Jacob's twin (Bib.)
49. Disgusting
50. Prima donna
51. Paradise
52. Object of worship
53. Wheel cushion
54. Slow-cooked dish
57. Drink like dog

PUZZLE 63

ACROSS

1. Small fruit seed
5. Move along ground
10. Biblical prophet
14. First man (Bib.)
15. Lodging place
16. Long live! (Sp.)
17. Perform alone
18. Knowing
19. Paradise
20. Sailing vessels
22. Province in China
24. Kitties
26. Jacob's twin (Bib.)
27. Illuminates
31. Helpful
35. Zodiac sign
36. Separately
38. Black cuckoo
39. Snatches (colloq.)
40. "__ and Prejudice"
41. Forbidding
42. Wind direction (abbr.)
43. Turned white
44. Greek island
45. Female sibling
47. Isolates
49. Rodents
51. Small alcoholic drink
52. Telling story of
56. Walked leisurely
60. Desertlike
61. Punctuation mark
63. Swinging stride
64. Evergreen tree
65. Parasitic insect
66. Level
67. Puts into position
68. Borders
69. Watches

DOWN

1. Move past
2. Object of worship
3. __ Alto, Calif.
4. Kisses and hugs (sl.)
5. Virtuous
6. Things in line
7. And others (2 wds., abbr.)
8. Uncanny
9. Delight
10. Street
11. Mid-calf length (comb.)
12. Microwave __
13. Warbled
21. Taps gently
23. Tobacco-drying kiln
25. Tangle

27. Narrow roads

28. Persian

29. Jeers

30. Secret agents

32. Got on

33. Join together

34. Greenish citrus fruits

37. Calculated total

40. Tiny fragment

41. Mutters discontentedly

43. Fuel from bogs

44. A shellfish

46. Exchanges

48. Wading birds

50. Baglike hair net

52. Knocks

53. Great Lake

54. Thread bits

55. Drink in gulps

57. Deep devotion

58. Fencing sword

59. Lairs

62. Carbohydrate (suff.)

PUZZLE 64

ACROSS

1. Acting against
5. Main artery
10. Military rank (abbr.)
13. Suppose
14. Salesman's pitch (sl.)
15. Chest sound
16. Region
17. Of the Pope
18. Mild oath
19. Dog of mixed breed
21. Way of access
23. Charged atom
24. A toast; "Here's __"(2 wds.)
25. Circular
28. Type of plane
29. Meat
33. Skin disease
34. Piece of butter
35. Canadian Indian
36. Wager
37. Virtuously
39. Small child
40. Jumped from plane; __ out
42. Bob the head
43. We are (contr.)
44. Waterway
45. Carry with effort
46. Nest dwellers
47. Records
49. Came in first

50. Became permanent
53. Horrible
57. Have concern for
58. Nimble
60. Buckeye State
61. Above
62. Hope chest wood
63. Bill of fare
64. Tiny
65. Wear away
66. Ogled

DOWN

1. __ and Eve
2. Roman fiddler
3. Adolescent
4. Make a mental picture
5. Ski resort
6. Type of gem
7. Tear
8. "Tempest in a __"
9. Put to rest; ease one's mind
10. Heroic story
11. National banner
12. Give up; yield
15. Outcome
20. __ and reel
22. Physically weak person
24. Bacterial disease producing
     muscular spasms
25. Jewish leader

26. Pacific or Atlantic
27. Up to then
28. Jolt
30. "Peter, Peter, pumpkin ___"
31. Long bladed weapon
32. Detests
34. Pea container
35. Ancient
37. Ore ingredient
38. Fireplace wood
41. Written message
43. Charming

45. Book of records
46. Large snake
48. Tranquility
49. In what place
50. Type of boat
51. Roof edge
52. Bird nest site
53. Happy
54. These people
55. Row
56. You would (contr.)
59. Wedding words

PUZZLE 65

ACROSS

1. Take by sudden grasp
5. Band leader's wand
10. Resound
14. Lion's den
15. Wear away
16. George Bernard __
17. Alan __; actor
18. Fence openings
19. Quote
20. Tell about in detail
22. Drew; copied
24. Even (poet.)
25. Applaud
26. Kid's game; __ play
29. Trembled
33. Wild west show
34. Emit light
35. Period of time
36. Landed
37. Informal vocabulary
38. Former ruler
39. New (comb.)
40. Tiny particles
41. The ones here
42. Calculate; guess
44. Arranged
45. For males
46. Self

47. Insist
50. Site
55. Eager; avid
56. Over
58. Honest
59. Roy Rogers and __ Evans
60. Behaved violently
61. Not as much
62. Chances
63. Male bee
64. Time zone (abbr.; pl.)

DOWN

1. Very willing
2. Chest sound
3. Assists
4. Wrist band
5. Starts
6. Camel rider
7. Carry
8. Type of poem
9. Baby bird
10. Get free
11. Stylish
12. Detest
13. Was in debt
21. Decorate again
23. Rant
25. Facial features

26. Type of stork
27. Perforations
28. Stupid one
29. Disgrace
30. Change the clock
31. Rub out
32. Challenged
34. Coin openings
37. Typical
38. Choke
40. Prayer ending
41. Roman garment

43. Likenesses
44. Withdraw formally
47. Grooving tool
48. Mild oath
49. Shaping device
50. Motto
51. Baking chamber
52. Angers
53. Remove from office
54. Loch __ monster
57. Prevent from entering

PUZZLE 66

ACROSS

1. Fail to perform
5. Rope loop
10. Small boy
13. Beside (pref.)
14. Central
15. Domesticate
16. __ Alda; actor
17. Hand covering
18. Press
19. Long
21. Bliss
23. Destiny
24. As late as
25. Light weapon
28. __ and outs
29. Oozes
33. Greek god of war
34. Flightless bird
35. Horseman's seat
36. Born
37. Uppermost dirt
39. Gosh
40. Cardboard box
42. Middle East federation (abbr.)
43. Peruse
44. Treatise
45. Feline
46. Bird homes
47. Make merry

49. Large
50. Mortification
53. Hinted
57. Possess
58. Make amends
60. Ear part
61. Landed
62. Salamanders
63. Quickly
64. Scarlet
65. Don clothing
66. Lease

DOWN

1. Gem with delicate colors
2. Masculine
3. Persia
4. Muddles
5. Evening
6. Just
7. Yoko __; singer
8. Lucky numbers
9. Build
10. Scarlett's home
11. __ and Andy
12. Gainsay
15. Named
20. Peak
22. Fiber plant
24. Strange

25. Spear
26. Regions
27. Fortune tellers
28. Little devil
30. Borders
31. Fabric fold
32. Plant "eggs"
34. Long time
35. Knight's title
37. Trifler
38. Cereal grain
41. Bull's eye
43. Normal

45. Midpoint
46. Nothing
48. Article of food
49. Consecrate
50. Burn
51. Healthy
52. Eager
53. Picnic pests
54. Finished
55. Black
56. Depression
59. Be indebted to

PUZZLE #1

T	A	N	S		C	O	R	A	L		R	A	T	A
A	L	O	E		A	L	O	N	E		E	G	A	D
L	A	S	T		R	E	A	D	S		V	A	L	E
C	R	E	A	T	I	O	N		S	T	O	R	E	S
			S	O	N			R	E	E	L			
R	A	C	I	N	G		D	E	N	A	T	U	R	E
E	V	A	D	E		S	I	D	E	S		N	U	N
N	A	M	E		S	T	A	I	D		P	I	N	T
D	I	E		H	E	A	R	D		D	O	T	E	R
S	L	O	V	E	N	L	Y		H	E	R	E	S	Y
			O	R	A	L		O	F	T				
M	A	S	C	O	T		P	E	N	T	A	G	O	N
A	R	I	A		O	L	I	V	E		B	O	N	O
C	E	L	L		R	A	K	E	S		L	O	C	O
E	A	T	S		S	P	E	N	T		E	D	E	N

PUZZLE #2

S	C	A	N		R	E	W	E	D		P	L	A	N
T	O	R	E		E	R	O	S	E		R	O	L	E
A	N	T	E	A	T	E	R	S		D	E	B	A	R
Y	E	S		L	I	C	K		M	E	S	S	E	D
			P	O	R	T		B	A	L	E			
D	E	F	I	N	E		R	E	L	A	T	I	V	E
A	R	O	S	E		J	E	L	L	Y		M	I	A
L	A	N	A		S	E	A	L	S		P	A	L	S
E	S	T		S	H	A	P	E		B	U	G	L	E
S	E	S	S	I	O	N	S		R	E	P	E	A	L
			I	D	E	S		B	O	S	S			
S	T	A	L	L	S		B	O	U	T		M	I	G
H	A	L	V	E		C	L	A	S	S	M	A	T	E
E	R	S	E		H	O	U	S	E		A	M	E	N
D	O	O	R		P	O	E	T	S		T	A	M	E

PUZZLE #3

W	A	R	E		B	A	S	E	S		S	H	A	M
E	V	E	N		A	G	E	N	T		H	A	M	E
S	E	N	D		L	E	A	S	E		R	T	E	S
T	R	O	U	B	L	E	S		A	L	I	E	N	S
			R	E	O			E	D	E	N			
S	P	R	I	N	T		D	R	I	N	K	I	N	G
P	R	I	N	T		F	I	N	E	S		D	E	R
R	U	N	G		R	I	T	E	S		G	E	R	E
A	N	D		K	E	E	T	S		C	R	A	V	E
Y	E	S	A	N	D	N	O		C	O	I	L	E	D
			N	E	E	D		H	I	D				
B	U	L	G	E	S		S	C	A	N	D	A	L	S
O	R	A	L		I	O	T	A	S		L	U	A	U
O	G	R	E		G	R	O	P	E		E	R	I	E
R	E	D	S		N	E	W	E	R		S	A	N	D

PUZZLE #4

S	T	O	P		D	O	W	E	R		R	O	B	S
L	A	N	A		I	R	A	T	E		A	G	R	A
A	P	E	S		V	E	N	A	L		F	L	A	G
M	E	S	S	I	E	S	T		E	F	F	E	T	E
			I	R	S			N	A	I	L			
A	F	L	O	A	T		F	O	S	T	E	R	E	D
I	R	O	N	S		B	L	U	E	S		E	R	A
S	I	P	S		S	O	U	N	D		S	L	A	T
L	E	E		E	T	O	N	S		N	O	I	S	E
E	S	S	A	Y	I	N	G		C	O	P	T	E	R
			P	E	L	E		H	A	P				
E	L	A	P	S	E		B	E	E	H	I	V	E	S
M	I	L	L		T	R	A	D	E		E	A	V	E
I	S	L	E		T	A	L	E	S		S	N	E	E
R	A	Y	S		O	P	I	N	E		T	E	N	D

PUZZLE #5

S	E	C	S		B	R	E	A	D		R	E	T	S
A	X	L	E		L	O	D	G	E		E	V	I	L
L	A	U	D		A	S	S	E	T		T	E	L	E
E	M	B	A	L	M	S		E	A	R	N	E	D	
			T	I	E		L	A	R	G	E			
A	I	D	E	S		S	O	L		O	A	S	I	S
O	D	E		T	R	A	U	M	A		T	U	N	A
R	E	B		S	A	L		O	R	B		G	A	L
T	A	I	L		N	A	U	S	E	A		A	N	T
A	L	T	E	R		D	S	T		C	A	R	E	S
			G	E	E	S	E		C	O	D			
A	R	M	A	D	A		S	U	N	D	I	A	L	
C	O	O	L		R	O	V	E	R		L	O	D	E
I	D	O	L		T	R	I	A	L		E	W	E	S
D	E	N	Y		H	E	E	L	S		S	A	S	S

PUZZLE #6

C	L	O	D		G	L	U	E	D		R	O	W	S
R	A	G	E		L	A	S	S	O		E	V	I	L
O	I	L	S		A	D	A	P	T		C	A	R	E
P	R	E	P	A	R	E		T	A	I	L	E	D	
			O	D	E		T	R	Y	S	T			
P	H	O	T	O		W	E	E		K	E	E	P	S
R	E	P		P	A	R	A	D	E		S	N	I	P
I	R	E		T	I	E		S	E	A		T	V	A
M	O	R	E		L	A	B	O	R	S		E	O	N
E	N	A	C	T		T	U	X		P	A	R	T	S
			O	A	T	H	S		A	I	D			
G	O	I	N	G	S		I	N	C	H	I	N	G	
A	L	T	O		A	M	O	N	G		E	R	I	A
S	I	A	M		R	A	N	G	E		R	O	L	L
H	O	L	Y		S	T	E	E	R		E	N	E	S

PUZZLE #7

```
SCOT  SLATE    TRA
LODI  HARES   SWIG
AVON  OMENS   PILE
MERGERS   DAMAGES
      LOT FOYER
LADEN  FUN  TEASE
ARES  PIT  PADDLE
MON  NATURAL  DOR
ASTRAL  ROW  YETI
RESET  RED  WORSE
     MATES LOU
REVILES   BANNERS
ODIN  RUBIK  GROW
BEND  SLAKE  ELLA
ENE   ETHER  RELY
```

PUZZLE #8

```
ALGA   TOAD  OMAR
SEAS  GOUGE  TORE
HIGHBUTTONSHOES
ESS  RIAS   PENS
      GILL ODOR
ASSIST   RAISED
STARK  TRAIL  MID
KILL  DIETS  GERE
SRO  SALVE  LUNGE
SNEEZE   CINDER
    LIES  CUBS
OFOZ  JURY   ILK
CARPENTERSAPRON
OTOE  AISLE  TONE
DHMS  BETS   ANEW
```

PUZZLE #9

```
RAFT  PLAIT  CLAD
ECRU  LANCE  LICE
DEER  ASTER  ANNE
OSTRICH   RISKED
     ERE GEARS
SANTA  HEX  KEEPS
OLE  TOILED  DART
ROE  ERA RUE  SUE
ENDS  STATED  ENE
RESTS  UPS  IDLED
     RAISE RTE
STRAPS   BUSTLES
IRAN  SAPID  AONE
FIND  UNITE  IRON
TOTS  EAGER  NEST
```

PUZZLE #10

```
DOPE   PUNS  ELSE
AVER  BATIK  LOAN
MARRIAGELICENSE
ELK  TIES   AVES
     WELD LOPE
TOTEMS   EVENTS
OPALS  SEVER  EAT
TILL  UTTER  GALE
ONO  TRACE  ARSON
ENERGY   FRIEND
     LIES HIED
ALEC   EARN  PTA
TRICKORTREATERS
RIFT  DOORS  ATOP
IDES  DENY   GETS
```

PUZZLE #11

```
TWAS  SMITE  CHET
HALE  WADER  HARE
ASEA  INANE  ELSA
THERAPY   CRATER
     EVE GETUP
SLIDE  SAX  BLEAR
HID  RANGED  YMCA
ABE  TIE MIG  MUG
FRAT  DAMPEN  ATE
TALES  KIT  ASSES
     TRESS BRO
ANCHOR   HALIBUT
FIRE  RATER  LENA
ALAR  OCEAN  EATS
REBS  REEDS  DUOS
```

PUZZLE #12

```
SAGE   SODA  AFEW
OGLE  COMIC  SAGA
FOURTHDIMENSION
AGE  ROOT   AIRS
      HARM OHMS
SESAME   MEETUP
CLUMP  TREAD  NAP
ODES  POUND  SAUL
WED  LIKES  TORSO
RECIPE   FOAMED
     AMEN FLOP
JAMB   BRAT  SEA
TIMEONYOURHANDS
EVIL  EERIE  PUGH
TEDS  WANT   OBEY
```

PUZZLE #13

```
APER  SHEEP  SADE
MALE  LEAVE  MEOW
ORBS  EASED  OOZE
SEATBELT  IRONER
   LIP    SCOT
COMETS  SOUTHERN
AMASS  SPARE  LEE
NABS  ALIKE  BABE
SHE  KNEES  BATED
TALENTED  PURELY
   JILT    HOE
DELETE  AWAYWITH
EXEC  RAVES  IDEA
LINT  ELOPE  REST
ETAS  DENTS  ESTE
```

PUZZLE #14

```
SEAL  ADEPT  SLED
TRUE  GUSTO  PELE
AIRS  IDEAL  RASE
REASONS   LOAFER
   ERG    ASSAY
ARENA  DDT  TEPID
WAR  THESIS  DONE
ADE  EON  NRA  USN
RICH  BONGOS  RES
DOTED  TOY  TASTE
   AUGER   BET
PISTOL   DIRTIES
ROTH  AWAIT  ENVY
OTOE  SOLES  STEN
DAWN  SEEDY  TORE
```

PUZZLE #15

```
GARB  BRASS   NAB
ALOE  LUNCH  HERO
MEAL  ENSUE  EATS
EERIEST  REBATES
   ENS    ERROR
ALIVE  PAY  ASHES
LIME  MAR  BREAST
EVA  PENNIES  SSA
REGION  END  STAR
TRESS  ASK  ANEYE
   LEAST    LIE
PARADES  CAREFUL
AMEN  ROBOT  ZONE
PIED  IRATE  ERIE
ADD  ETHER  SETS
```

PUZZLE #16

```
SCAB  DATES  TSAR
AURA  EXILE  INRE
GREG  LEMON  TACT
STAPLE  EPITAPHS
   IOTA    ELAN
CHAPTERS  INSIST
ROPES  MASTS  NCO
UMPS  DOLLY  SPAN
MEL  SERVE  INURE
BREAKS  OPERATES
   DIPS    TROT
PLEASING  ANCHOR
LAMP  SEALS  HIVE
ADIT  EERIE  EDEN
NETS  DRYER  DENT
```

PUZZLE #17

```
LATE  BATON  BEST
OMEN  AWARE  ERIE
ABED  LENDS  SINE
FINEST  SETTINGS
   ACID    READ
TERRACES  GREASE
ALIEN  PANGS  SAN
MILD  LOGOS  SPUD
ETE  BITES  PIECE
DESPOT  RETURNED
   RATA    SELL
DEBATERS  SLOPED
OMIT  ROOST  IOTA
DIKE  EMOTE  NORM
ORES  DATER  SHES
```

PUZZLE #18

```
LEND   OWLS   RAVE
OBOE  STEEP  ERIN
NOTWITHSTANDING
ENE  MEET   IDLE
   LAIR   RACE
ASSIGN   EVENTS
CHIVE  FLAIR  RAH
HARE  TIERS  JIVE
ERE  LONGS  DETER
ENSURE   BREEDS
   PROD   SOAR
ERIE  ATOM   ERG
STANDARDIZATION
ROTE  SIDLE  ARIA
ONES  HOSE   BELT
```

```
HERB   MOATS   OMEN
ALEE   YACHT   RAGE
LANG   STEER   ERGS
ONTIME   SMALLEST
    NILS   ENOS
TRANSFER   GREASE
HALES   LOVED   VAN
ODOR   FLAIR   BALD
RIO   PASSE   ALIVE
NOFAIR   TRAVELED
   SETA   SPIN
SNAPSHOT   ADDLED
HAVE   ERECT   EERY
AMEN   STASH   RALE
MESS   TASTY   SPED
```

```
HAHA   CAPRI   BOOM
OVER   ALIAS   OGRE
NORMALITY   SALES
EWE   ELKS   THRESH
    ISEE   GRID
TERROR   TRANSACT
SNOOP   PROPS   PAY
ASSN   DRAWS   HARP
RUE   DOOMS   CURVE
SESSIONS   BASTES
    HARE   BASH
TAPERS   SORT   CPA
ARRAY   THRESHOLD
LEER   CRUEL   ALOE
LASS   CINDY   METS
```

```
LOFT   MESA   METS
ARIA   DARES   EDIT
CARRYINGCHARGES
ELM   EGOS   LIES
   HAIR   TROT
REPORT   RINSED
EARNS   LEASE   VAT
AGOG   WINCE   RENO
DEN   RIVET   SANTA
  REPOSE   PARTED
   AMES   BALE
  FORE   SIRE   CAR
LINEOFSCRIMMAGE
OVEN   LOADS   AMEN
WEST   ANTS   NEST
```

```
MAD   CAP   AMP
ALIT   MODEL   GLEE
ROAR   INANE   ASEA
  ELECTS   CARROT
   NUT   DINED
CODE   OIL   MEAT
MAPS   BAG   HINGES
ODE   TURNOUT   ANT
PERIOD   IRE   CITY
TASK   ATE   SONS
  LEERY   PET
MOANER   TATTLE
COIN   LOCAL   OOPS
POND   SWARM   NOEL
ASK   STA   KEY
```

```
SOFA   DECOY   JAPE
AMEN   ELIDE   URAL
VENTILATE   BLINK
ENS   CUTE   BRIDGE
   MODE   CLUE
REFINE   FLUTTERS
AMISS   FLARE   RAT
COLT   FOAMS   CODE
ETE   PORTS   MADAM
DESSERTS   COVERS
   TRAY   MATE
GREASY   CANE   ATE
LORNE   CONCLUDED
AVID   MOOSE   SARD
DENS   YOKEL   EMMY
```

```
PLOY   LACE   GILL
LOPE   SENOR   ALOE
ONEARMEDBANDITS
DEN   AIRY   AGES
   WILY   GAVE
DEPOSE   ELATES
ADORE   FINAL   VIA
LIKE   HIRES   BEEP
ICE   FARES   PURGE
TRILLS   BARTER
   NYET   BENT
DOVE   TOAD   SEE
SUPERABUNDANTLY
ONUS   CONES   EASE
BEST   EWER   BRAD
```

PUZZLE #25

```
CALM CRAVE EIRE
OBOE HUMAN URAL
SLAM AGENT RANK
TENORS SERPENTS
    RATE SALK
ENTIRELY NEARER
BOOZE AORTA ELI
BONE ANKAS CROP
ESE ENDED SHAPE
DESIGN LISTENER
    NOON OLES
REISSUES ETHICS
ANTI NIECE IDOL
IDES CLASP REDO
LOST ESSAY EAST
```

PUZZLE #26

```
BRAD CITE RADAR
RALE OVEN ELOPE
IVAN LINE SOLED
NEMO LED SPEEDS
KNOTTED ROE
    ERG CINCTURE
WOK YEARN TOTED
ALEE SMASH MEND
SEEKS IBEAM STY
HOPELESS ROD
    ENS SPEAKER
ATTEND COO MODE
LURID SOLO ARIA
SNORE ELAN GEED
OATER TARS EASY
```

PUZZLE #27

```
DOFF SLAB PLOY
ABED CHILE ROLE
FOURWHEELDRIVES
TED REDS ONES
    PEAS PLOT
LATENT LOTSOF
AMASS TRAPS RIN
MUST SHINE VANE
EST ETUDE HATES
EYELID MISERS
    AIRS FADE
TEST RAKE WEE
THREEPIECESUITS
ROLL INNER SLAP
ARES ENOS ALLY
```

PUZZLE #28

```
ALAR DOSE RILED
DOLE INTO ERASE
AVON STAN PASTE
PENT TAR CENTER
TREETOP BAN
    DOR LETTERED
ADE ETHER STOVE
DEEP SAVED ASEA
ALLAH DETER END
MISNOMER FIT
    LAS MEMOIRS
REPAST HER ANEW
ADOPT MOTE SURE
TENSE OPEN TRUE
SNEER PERT SENT
```

PUZZLE #29

```
ARTS PALES SHED
BEAU ALERT CAKE
LAMP RANGE RHEA
ELEPHANT ABOARD
    LAD IDOL
ENGINE DRILLERS
LINED DEALT BET
BEAS SALTY PONE
OCT PEWEE DONEE
WESTERNS SAWYER
    RAGS ITE
BEWARE REGARDED
ARID ACORN FIDO
LIFE NOOSE UNIT
LEES TOTED LETS
```

PUZZLE #30

```
TOMS SLIP SPUD
AREA ATONE LARD
CARLSBADCAVERNS
OLE POLE OUTS
    HAUL SUIT
ABSENT ARCHES
COALS MANGE PTS
CRUD BASTE HEAT
TEN TAMPA QUERY
SAHARA PURSES
    EBBS SLOT
HALO SLAT CIO
YELLOWSTONEPARK
AMMO ELOPE AFAR
MOSS TYPE LENA
```

PUZZLE #31

```
SALT  RITE  MOLAR
ODOR  EMIT  AROMA
NOSE  GALA  RAVEN
AREA  AGE   SILENT
RESTORE    SON
      SAD   MODERATE
IRA   REBEL ROMAN
DOVE  DOLES BIRD
OMENS NESTS DES
SERENADE   RIG
      EDS   RATRACE
SCARED FIN  ALOW
LABOR WING  DIME
AMUSE ELSE  EVER
METED DEER  SETS
```

PUZZLE #32

```
EMIT  PURE  BEOFF
NAME  USES  ARGUE
AJAR  RULE  NARES
COGS  PRY   EASELS
TREETOP     MEN
      RRS   BALANCED
APE   YEARN SERVE
TADS  DRAIN TEEN
ORATE STAIN WRY
MEMENTOS    MID
      DEN   OBLIGES
AVENUE SOL  ELAN
VIGOR HAZE  SAGE
OVATE ONES  ERLE
WADED TEST  LEER
```

PUZZLE #33

```
SLOW  LOSES HAM
HAVE  ADORE ROVE
ONES  POLAR ALES
PARTNER     SURFERS
      EEL   REMIT
SCARE BUD   DECAL
TORN  BUS   BERATE
AVE   GENTLER SON
RENTED LIT  SEND
STARE LED   CEDES
      ASTER SAN
GLIDERS     PIRATES
LODE  ASPEN TIRE
ARES  CEASE ODIE
DES   ENDOW REED
```

PUZZLE #34

```
SANG  SPAT  RED
AREA  TRIED MULE
LAWS  RIDER ESSE
ELF   KIDS  ERASED
      OLIVE HAITI
GUISE HAMS  ARE
PONDS MORSE NAG
LADS  ARM   BRIG
ELL   BLISS FOOLS
ASA   RAZE  BONUS
      NOISE MOREL
PADRES LIST END
ALDA  OPENS STOA
COOL  SINCE ATOM
KEG   TOES  PENS
```

PUZZLE #35

```
ODOR  ARCH  MINI
RODE  DRAPE ARID
GODBLESSAMERICA
YRS   ATOP  VISE
      AMEN  SPIN
DAUBER      LILACS
INNER QUITS APE
ADIT  OUSTS ANEW
LET   SPIES ALONE
SELLER      BREEDS
      OINK  JAGS
SPAN  TUTU  FLU
PLEDGETOTHEFLAG
RATE  SPREE FELL
OWED  EKES  AWAY
```

PUZZLE #36

```
ERA   FOB   HOE
LARD  CAPES CAWS
KNEW  OCTET HINT
TSETSE      TUBERS
      LOT   ELDER
MOLE  AXE   AURA
JAMS  TIC   AMBUSH
AYE   INDIANS MII
YOGURT TRY  MODE
RANK  PET   BARE
      TEPID SOT
GLIDER      HEARSE
ALOE  GAVEL OURS
LEAD  STIFF NEST
GEM   EAT   SEE
```

PUZZLE #37

```
P O E T   R O M P S   E V E R
A N T E   U N I O N   L I N E
I C O N   S E N S E   A N T I
L E N S E S   T E A S P O O N
      I R I S   S K I S
C O L O R A N T   E R E C T S
E V A N S   A W A R E   A R I
D U N S   U R A L S   C U E D
A L E   U N L I T   P A S S E
R E S E T S   N A M E L E S S
      N E T S   R O L L
P L E A S A N T   U T U R N S
L A M B   B A I T S   P A U L
E V I L   L I N U S   O T T O
D A T E   E L A T E   N E S T
```

PUZZLE #38

```
A C T     D E S     D A D
S H A M   F I R E S   T I L E
H A R I   L E G A L   I V A N
  P A R R O T   M I S T E R
        R U G   P E T A L
  I R O N   S O D   T E A M
O D O R   B U T   H I D D E N
W E B   M E N T I O N   D O E
N A I L E D   E V E   N E W T
  S N I T   C R Y   C A R S
      T A L L Y   D A B
  A Z A L E A   R O B O T S
O P E N   N I N E S   B E A D
V E R Y   S M I L E   S A G E
A D O     S P Y     R A W
```

PUZZLE #39

```
P R O P   H A V E N   T H O R
E A V E   A L O N E   H O P E
T R A P E Z O I D   F I N A L
E E L   L A N D   B A R E L Y
      B U R G   D E N S
M I S A D D   P R A C T I C E
I R A T E   R O O M Y   N O R
D O T S   W E L L S   L A V A
A N Y   G A V E L   T I N E S
S Y R I N G E S   C H E E S E
      N O E L   W H E N
C H A S M S   L A I R   D U O
R U P E E   P O N D E R I N G
A G E R   C A R T E   E V I L
B E S T   D R E S S   F E T E
```

PUZZLE #40

```
M I S T   A L O F T   E M M A
E C H O   N E W E R   M A I L
T O I L   N A N N Y   P Y L E
E N V E L O P   O R I O L E
      D A Y   M I N E R
R O B O T   R I N   F E A S T
I R A   I D E A L S   S O H O
N A G   N I P   A I M   R E G
S T E P   M A R I N E   T E A
E E L E R   S O D   D E A N S
      N U T T Y   O I L
B E R A T E   A C C E P T S
E T A L   P O A C H   V A S E
S U I T   I N N E R   E L A N
T I D Y   D E N S E   N E R D
```

PUZZLE #41

```
A P E S   R E A P   S A F E R
M A X I   E R G O   O L I V E
A N T E   F R E E   M U L E S
S I R S   L O S   C E M E N T
S C A T T E R   S A D
      A R C   S T R A I G H T
E S T   I T A L Y   Y O Y O S
D O U R   S T A L E   U P U P
A S T A S   T I E R S   S R S
M O U N T A I N   U S E
      E T C   S P E N C E R
S E T T E E   S I T   T A L E
T R A I L   M I N I   E R I N
U N C L E   O L E O   R A T E
D E T E R   D O W N   S T E W
```

PUZZLE #42

```
S P I N   P E E L   C H A N T
L O R E   R E D O   H A N O I
U S E S   E R A S   E L T O N
M E N T   T I M   T A L E N T
P R E L A T E   T A P
      E L I   B E N E F I T S
C U P   L E M O N   R A T I O
A T O P   R O L E S   T E E N
P A N E S   O T T E R   M R S
S H Y S T E R S   M O P
      A Y E   F E D E R A L
B E W A R E   G A S   T O L E
E V E R T   M O L T   I D L E
A E R I E   E R S E   T E A K
T R E A D   L E E R   E O N S
```

PUZZLE #43

```
PAPA  CLOSE    LOG
ICED  HAITI   RIDE
TRAM  IDLED   IRON
SERIALS  WELFARE
    RID  FERAL
SPEAR  POD  TEASE
TALL  HUN  TESTER
ATE  HANDLER  TIN
RICHES  LEA  SIZE
TOTAL  BET  FACES
    PLEAD  NEW
SUPPORT  SUNDAES
ISLE  OTTER  UNDO
DEAN  SLAMS  STEP
EST  EERIE  TENS
```

PUZZLE #44

```
OTIC  SWANS   HALE
WHOO  PAINT   AMID
LAWN  ORDER   WOVE
STATIONS  AWAKEN
     INN   VIII
STINKS  CANNIBAL
MINUS  RULED  ADO
IDLE  TABOR  CROP
LEE  SEVER  ELOPE
ESTEEMED  SCENTS
    LAPS   TRA
INSULT  ABOUNDED
SEED  IGLOO  SORE
LONE  NASAL  ELLA
ENDS  GROSS  DEER
```

PUZZLE #45

```
CALF  RACE   TEPEE
ODOR  ELAN   IVORY
LOCO  VINE   TENSE
ORAL  IKE   SANDED
RELIEVE   PAN
    CPA  SINISTER
ART  ALONE  CHORE
JOIN  SLICE  ERIE
ALLOT  IDEAL  END
RETRIEVE  RID
    LEE  KNEADED
AWHILE  POI  NEAR
WHITE  BURN  CAGE
EIDER  BRAG  ELLA
DRESS  BENS  STEM
```

PUZZLE #46

```
RING  PROSE  PEAT
AREA  LEASE  LALA
ROAR  ENTER  ERAL
ENTREAT   ITALIC
    EAT  LEERS
DEBTS  SEA  YEAST
ARE  ENTIRE  DIME
TAR  LEO  NAP  DIN
USES  ORDERS  ETE
METER  MID  ASSET
    VERSE  PLY
SLEEVE   MAMMALS
HAIR  PETAL  BLOC
OKRA  EVADE  OTTO
PEEL  LATER  LOST
```

PUZZLE #47

```
ELSE    COPE   TRAY
SOUL  SUGAR   RITE
PUBLICRELATIONS
YDS  DOSE   IPSO
    TILE   AFRO
RAMROD   NEEDLE
OPIUM  LOWED  EAT
MARE  TIDAL  MAGI
ART  BAKER  LISLE
    THRICE  BARTER
    IRON  VOTE
CANT   KINE   OAT
FLIGHTINSURANCE
RUDE  OLEOS  CENT
YEAR  PEER   TREE
```

PUZZLE #48

```
SHOD  CLAPS  DUMP
COVE  HELLO  ESAU
APES  IDLER  TEST
MENTAL   ARRESTS
    RIDES   YES
GROOM  LAS  STRAP
HOLY  MULLET  EGO
ODD  DAD  EOS  GAR
SEE  UNEVEN  TAPE
TORTE  SIP  SALES
    ATE  ASSET
CLASSIC   ATTACH
ROBS  DONOR  ERLE
EPEE  ELAND  REAR
WELL  RAGES  SANE
```

PUZZLE #49

```
A L A S   U S A G E       L P S
D E N T   N U D E S     B O R E
D A T E   I R O N S     E C O L
S P I N O F F   D A S H O F F
      C R Y   K E Y T O
C U T I E   S I R   A O R T A
A B E L   H I S   O F F E R S
R O N   C U T S O F F   S A T
T A S T E D   O A T   W A D E
S T E A L   O F F   L O W E R
      C L I F F   G E L
K I C K O F F   G O O F O F F
E V I L   N I T R O   I S L E
N A T E   O C E A N   S H O E
O N E     T E E M S   H A G S
```

PUZZLE #50

```
C H A R   C A L L   S A T A N
L U R E   O R E S   A G I L E
O M I T   L E N D   T E P E E
N A S A   L A S   M I S S E D
E N E M I E S   S I S
      E T C   H A L F L I F E
H A S   S T R A W   Y E M E N
E L L A   S A T E D   A P E D
M A I L S   S E D A N   S T S
P I T S T O P S   M A T
      E L S   A P P E A R S
T R A D E D   A D E   A S E A
R O T O R   E B O N   S I L L
A T O N E   M E R E   E D I T
M O P E D   S L E D   S E T S
```

PUZZLE #51

```
R O W       C O D       S P A
A V I D   F A R E D   D E A R
M E R E   A R E N A   E A S T
  R E C I T E   O T H E R S
      A C E   S T E A M
  S I D E   A W E   T E N S
F A M E   A G O   R E D U C E
A V A   S P E L L E D   D O W
R E G A L E   L A D   O G R E
  D E L E   F E W   T R E E
      L E M O N   W A D
  L O O T E D   A R R E S T
S E A T   A D A G E   R E A M
E A R S   T E N O N   S A L E
A D S       R I G       L E T
```

PUZZLE #52

```
H A L     W A R       M A T
U N I T   P A R I S   W A G E
T E A R   A S C O T   I D E A
  W R E N C H   T A S T E S
      M A E   P E R C H
  H O O P   P A D   E E L S
P E A R   L E I   E N R I C H
E L K   E A R N E S T   O R O
G L E A N S   T A T   S N A P
  O N U S   B E T   G A S P
      T U B E R   R U B
  C O H E R E   D O N O R S
H O M O   A T L A S   T I N A
E V E R   G L A R E   S T O W
M E N     E Y E       E W E
```

PUZZLE 53

```
G E M       B E T       C O P
O X E N   B E A R D   M O V E
D I R E   E N T E R   A M E N
  T E S T E D   M A S T E R
      T O R   R O B O T
  H E L P   P E R   L E S T
S O L E   B A G   P A R T E D
A L I   M A R I N E R   A P O
P E T T E D   M U G   P R I M
  S E A L   H E N   W E E D
      S O L O N   P A W
  C A T N I P   C E N T E R
L A C E   S P A R E   E D A M
A R I D   T E N O R   R I T E
W E D       R I P       T E N
```

PUZZLE #54

```
H A R I   W A L E S   M A P S
E B O N   I R A T E   A L O E
W E P T   D E M U R   G E N E
S L E E V E   A D V A N C E D
      R A S P   E I R E
F O R E S T E R   T E T H E R
A R I S E   S I L O S   O N E
L I N T   M O T O R   C U T E
L O G   B A S E D   E A S E D
S N O R E D   S E T T L E R S
      E T O N   S A N E
P R O F A N E S   R A N D O M
L A M E   N I T E R   D E L I
A V E R   A G A T E   A M E N
Y E N S   S H R E D   R O S E
```

PUZZLE #55

R O B		S A P			H A L
U G L Y	S A L E S	D O V E
B L U E	T W I S T	U S E D
E R A S E S	T A M P E R
R A M	F E R A L
W A N T	F I R	G E R M
W A R S	M A N	P I X I E S
A I D	S A T A N I C	V A T
Y V O N N E	L A G	M A N Y
E R I E	S L Y	P A L S
N A S T Y	F A R
M E E K L Y	G A R B L E
P I N T	A L O U D	L A I R
A N D Y	T E R S E	E C R U
Y E S	S E T	K E N

PUZZLE #56

A D D	G E O	H A Y
N E A T	D I R G E	G A L E
D A T E	U R A L S	O R E S
D A N I E L	I T A L I C
N O T	S N A R E
S H I N	F O G	A M B I
A P E S	P A L	O B S E S S
D O A	P E R I O D S	E S S
S O D D E N	D A D	T R U E
L Y R E	E L K	D O S E
I V O R Y	T E A
G I V E R S	T O N S I L
C A V E	T A L O N	T O E D
O M A R	S T I R S	S T A R
B E N	Z E N	A N Y

PUZZLE #57

D A S H	G O R E S	S H I P
A L E E	A G E N T	T U N A
M A N X	G L A D E	A N T I
E N D A N G E R	E D I T O R
G A L	S P A R
A L C O V E	P A L I S A D E
C O R N Y	D A L E S	B E N
T O E S	D A R E S	F O N T
E S E	D E N I M	S O U S E
D E P L E T E S	C A R T E R
O N E S	O R E
G R U N T S	S P R I N T E R
R O P E	T A L O N	S I R E
I D O L	E V O K E	I R I S
D E N Y	D E T E R	C E N T

PUZZLE #58

L O P E	G L A D E	I V E S
O P A L	R O B I N	N I L E
V E N D	A D E P T	V E S T
E N T E N T E	E R A S E S
R O E	M I R E D
C R E S T	B E N	D E N I M
R E X	E V O L V E	D U D E
A V E	S I N	I W O	D E N
F U R S	M E L T E D	G A D
T E T O N	R Y E	D R E S S
L E A S E	P L O
B L A D E S	B A Y O N E T
R A N I	S A T I N	S A L E
A N T E	E L A T E	T I L E
T E A R	T I N E S	S L A M

PUZZLE #59

C L A P	S C O P E	S A L
R O D E	T A P E R	P I N E
A V E R	A F T E R	I N T O
M E S S A G E	V O Y A G E S
I C E	R E R U N
B E G A T	P O D	L O O S E
O M E N	S E A	P E S T E R
W O N	M I R R O R S	T I N
E T U D E S	I D O	G E N E
R E S E T	A N D	T I R E S
B E I N G	T A R
R E T U R N S	T H U D D E D
I V A N	A W A R E	L A V A
S I C K	N E V E R	E D E N
E L K	E R A S E	S A N E

PUZZLE #60

D J S	G A P	O H O
D E A D	O I L E D	S H I N
T E L E	D R A P E	P I N E
P E N C I L	P E R I O D
S O N	T E P I D
S H E D	E R R	T E L L
C H A R	A V A	A E R I A L
P A T	S H A M A N S	O R E
A D E P T S	P U T	I N K S
E S A U	I L K	T O S S
I N A N E	M O N
L E N S E S	M A R I N E
S E N T	R I D E S	Z E A L
P A D S	O D O R S	E A S Y
A D S	E W E	R T E

PUZZLE #61

```
F R O G   S T A M P   C A L M
E A V E   T U T O R   A L E E
A L A N   A N O D E   R O A R
T E L E G R A M   C H E E S E
      R A T     L E E S
S C R A P S   S I D E S T E P
E L I T E   M I N E D   A L E
R O V E   A I R E D   T R O T
U S E   O L D E R   G R O P E
M E R I D I A N   B O A T E R
      D O E S     A N I
C A V E R N   S T R E N G T H
A R I A   A W A I T   E R I E
R E E L   T I L D E   R I L L
P A S S   E N T E R   S T E P
```

PUZZLE #62

```
P R O M   P H O T O   C A R S
R A V E   R O G E R   U N I T
I C E D   O W L E T   R I T A
M E N D A B L E   H O L L E R
      L I E     S O M E
S H R E D S   S I D E W A L K
P E E R S   S A L O N   W I N
A L B S   P H L O X   S A T E
T I E   S L A T S   P U R E E
S O L I T A R Y   C A P E R S
      D I N E     A L P
R E V E R T   D E M E R I T S
A S I A   E L I D E   E D I T
M A L L   R A V E L   S O R E
S U E S   S P A N S   S L E W
```

PUZZLE #63

```
P I P S   C R E E P   A M O S
A D A M   H O T E L   V I V A
S O L O   A W A R E   E D E N
S L O O P S   L I A O N I N G
      C A T S   E S A U
L I G H T E N S   U S E F U L
A R I E S   A P A R T   A N I
N A B S   P R I D E   G R I M
E N E   P A L E D   C R E T E
S I S T E R   S E C L U D E S
      R A T S   D R A M
R E L A T I N G   A M B L E D
A R I D   C O L O N   L O P E
P I N E   L O U S E   E V E N
S E T S   E D G E S   S E E S
```

PUZZLE #64

```
A N T I   A O R T A     S F C
D E E M   S P I E L   R A L E
A R E A   P A P A L   E G A D
M O N G R E L   P A S S A G E
      I O N   T O Y O U
R O U N D   J E T   F L E S H
A C N E   P A T   O T T A W A
B E T   M O R A L L Y   T O T
B A I L E D   N O D   W E R E
I N L E T   L U G   B I R D S
      T A P E S   W O N
S E T T L E D   G H A S T L Y
C A R E   A G I L E   O H I O
O V E R   C E D A R   M E N U
W E E   E R O D E   E Y E D
```

PUZZLE #65

```
G R A B   B A T O N   E C H O
L A I R   E R O D E   S H A W
A L D A   G A T E S   C I T E
D E S C R I B E   T R A C E D
      E E N   C L A P
C H I L D S   S H I V E R E D
R O D E O   S H I N E   E R A
A L I T   S L A N G   T S A R
N E O   A T O M S   T H E S E
E S T I M A T E   S O R T E D
      M E N S   E G O
D E M A N D   L O C A T I O N
A G O G   A B O V E   T R U E
D A L E   R A G E D   L E S S
O D D S   D R O N E   E S T S
```

PUZZLE #66

```
O M I T   N O O S E     T A D
P A R A   I N N E R   T A M E
A L A N   G L O V E   I R O N
L E N G T H Y   E C S T A S Y
      L O T   U N T I L
L A S E R   I N S   S E E P S
A R E S   E M U   S A D D L E
N E E   T O P S O I L   G E E
C A R T O N   U A R   R E A D
E S S A Y   C A T   N E S T S
      R E V E L   B I G
C H A G R I N   A L L U D E D
H A V E   A T O N E   L O B E
A L I T   N E W T S   A N O N
R E D   D R E S S   R E N T
```